Loss Prevention Guide for Retail Businesses

The National Retail Federation Series

The National Retail Federation Series comprises books on retail store management, for stores of all sizes and for all management responsibilities. The National Retail Federation (NRF) is the world's largest retail trade association, with membership that includes the leading department, specialty, discount, mass merchandise, and independent stores, as well as 30 national and 50 state associations. NRF members represent an industry that encompasses more than 1.4 million U.S. retail establishments and employs nearly 20 million people—1 in 5 American workers. The NRF's international members operate stores in more than 50 nations.

The National Retail Federation Series includes:

Financial & Operating Results of Retail Stores in 1993,
     National Retail Federation
Merchandising & Operating Results of Retail Stores in 1993,
     National Retail Federation
Competing with the Retail Giants: How to Survive in the New Retail
     Landscape, *Kenneth E. Stone*
Value Retailing in the 1990s: Off-Pricers, Factory Outlets, and
     Closeout Stores, *Packaged Facts, Inc.*
Credit Card Marketing, *Bill Grady*
Loss Prevention Guide for Retail Businesses, *Rudolph C. Kimiecik*
Management of Retail Buying, 3rd edition, *R. Patrick Cash, John W.
     Wingate, and Joseph S. Friedlander*

Forthcoming Books:

Dictionary of Retailing and Merchandising, *Jerry M. Rosenberg*
Retail Store Planning & Design Manual, 2nd edition, *Michael Lopez*

Loss Prevention Guide for Retail Businesses

Rudolph C. Kimiecik

John Wiley & Sons, Inc.

New York • Chichester • Brisbane • Toronto • Singapore

Library of Congress Cataloging in Publication Data:

Kimiecik, Rudolph C.
    Loss prevention guide for retail businesses / Rudolph C. Kimiecik.
       p.   cm. — (National retail federation series)
    Includes bibliographical references.
    ISBN 0-471-07636-8 (acid-free paper)
    1. Retail trade—Security measures. 2. Shoplifting—Prevention.
  3. Employee theft—Prevention. 4. Fraud—Prevention. 5. Business
losses—Prevention. I. Title. II. Series.
HF5429.27.K55   1995
658.4\73—dc20   94-31723

Printed in the United States of America

10 9 8 7 6 5 4 3 2 1

To Retailers Everywhere
Purveyors of the necessities of life.

Preface

This book is based on a series of seminars given by the author, a Retail Security–Loss Prevention Specialist with over 35 years of professional experience. It covers a wide range of critical personal safety, physical security, and external and internal loss prevention subjects unique to the retail trade. Although intended especially as a guide for small and medium-size retailers without corporate security staffs, the book can also be extremely useful to large, multiunit retailers seeking to enhance and supplement existing in-house loss prevention practices.

The information, which is set forth in an informal, easy-to-understand format, is offered with but one purpose: to provide a much needed service to concerned retail store owners and managers. It is a totally unbiased presentation; the author has no financial interests or hidden tie-ins with any alarm companies, locksmiths, shopping services, or guard agencies. It is, in short, a plain and simple offering of genuine, understanding assistance.

RUDOLPH C. KIMIECIK

We once thought the world was flat.
Then round.
We now know that a lot of it
is crooked.

Anonymous
(But, undoubtedly, a retailer.)

Contents

Loss Prevention Guide for
Retail Businesses

INTRODUCTION

SCENARIO 1—MOONLIGHT MADNESS

It is two o'clock in the morning and the ringing of your bedside telephone jolts you out of a sound sleep. You answer, and the police tell you that the burglar alarm at your store has gone off, and they want you to come down. An officer will meet you there, so it can be checked out. So, mumbling to your significant other, you get dressed and go down to the store, right? Wrong! The first thing you do is call your servicing police department and verify that the call is legitimate, to ensure that you are not walking into a deadly trap.

SCENARIO 2—TAKE ME, TAKE ME!

You are very organized. You follow an established routine in running your store. Every day at about the same time you finalize your paperwork, gather up your receipts, put them in a bank deposit bag, and march off across the parking lot to your nearby bank. No problem,

1

right? Wrong! Unless you vary your times, camouflage that obvious bank bag (put it inside a store shopping bag), and have someone follow you at a discreet distance (to go for help in case you are held up, or to serve as a witness in case you are ever accused of fabricating a holdup), you are just begging to be robbed. And you will be.

SCENARIO 3—THE FLASHERS

Two well-dressed men come into your store and approach your young, part-time checkout clerk. They flash badges, state they are from the U.S. Secret Service, and say they are checking on a rash of reported counterfeit currency transactions in the area. They ask the clerk to open the cash register so they can examine all the 10s and 20s. She does and they do, periodically making check marks on a typewritten list of serial numbers they've brought with them, and laying a number of the bills to one side. When finished, they total up the bills laid aside, take them, and say to the clerk, "These bills are all counterfeit. As you know, we have to take them out of circulation. Here is a receipt for the amount we have taken; just give it to your manager, he will know what to do with it," and exit the store. All legitimate, right? Wrong! You have just been victimized by a couple of "con artists" who prey on naive, unaware, and untrained retail personnel.

SCENARIO 4—TAG, YOU'RE IT!

Finally, after months of suspicion that a woman customer is shoplifting, you see her stuff two silk scarves into her purse. You've finally got her. As she moves around the display and goes past another merchandise aisle, you can see her head and shoulders, and you note that she is rapidly moving toward an exit door. You rush to head her off and then confront her, right? Wrong, very wrong! Unless you can see the place of concealment from the time of the initial observation until the time of the confrontation—back off!! The suspect could have become concerned that she had been observed and ditched the scarves by hiding them under some other merchandise. She also could have switched purses with a passing accomplice whom you didn't even notice. By the time you stop her, she could be "clean." And then, depending on your comments and actions at the time of the confrontation, you could very well wind up being sued for false arrest, malicious prosecution, defamation of character, and so on. In fact, many so-called shoplifters make more money deliberately working this ploy than they do by actually stealing merchandise.

SCENARIO 5—HEADS I WIN, TAILS YOU LOSE!

Late on a busy Saturday afternoon in your hardware store, you are honored by a visit from "The Paint Man." Wearing suitably paint-spattered work clothes, he comes in, browses around for a bit, and then, when he determines that he is not being observed, removes two gallons of paint from your display. He then approaches your service counter and states, "Say, I really overestimated when I bought this paint here last week. I have a couple of gallons left over. Can you give me a refund? I looked for my receipt but I couldn't find it. It must have gotten thrown out when I was cleaning up." Informed that store policy prohibits a refund without a sales receipt, he then asks if he can exchange "his" two gallons for a couple of gallons in another color, because his wife now wants him to paint the bedrooms. That usually works, but if it doesn't, he plays his ace. "Well, I guess I can always use these for touch-up and maybe for doing some other rooms. Take care, I'll see you." He then strolls out of the store with two gallons of your paint. And you can rest assured that he didn't take your economy brand; he got your premium, $28-a-gallon, one-coat-covers, top-of-the-line product. Congratulations, you are now eligible for entry into the not so exclusive Paint Man Victim's Club. This scam is one of the oldest refund fraud games around. It has countless variations and has been adapted to work with a variety of products.

SCENARIOS 6, 7, AND 8—JUST TRUST ME!

You have a very hard-working floorman/janitor. He really keeps the sales floor clean and neat, and picks up the trash a lot. Unfortunately along with the trash, he also picks up valuable merchandise such as watches and cameras, which he throws into the dumpster out back and recovers at night after the store is closed.

Your super sales clerk always has a lot of traffic in her department and past her cash register. A lot of customers. Surprise, surprise . . . many of those customers are relatives and very close friends to whom she gives "personal" discounts and to whom she "slides" extra merchandise that they later split.

And don't forget that overworked cosmetician—you know, the one who comes in after her day job and brings in a softer pair of shoes to wear on the sales floor. When leaving at the end of the evening, she has a $75 bottle of perfume secreted in the toes of those very same shoes.

HOW THIS BOOK CAN HELP YOU

These are just a few examples of the countless ways you cannot only lose your money and your business, but risk your personal safety as well.

Such losses can be prevented by the development and implementation of a successful loss prevention program. First, however, you must develop a loss prevention state-of-mind; you must become aware of loss prevention, learn all you can about it, develop policies and procedures to support it, and then put a complete program into effect.

Start by identifying your vulnerabilities. To stop a leak, you have to know where the piping is faulty. This book has been written and structured to acquaint you with the full spectrum of retail loss prevention concerns. Without using any complex, technical jargon, it provides you with as much helpful and practical information as possible so that you may, in turn, create a program specifically tailored to meet your own needs.

The book is divided into logical, subjective chapters that cover the full spectrum of the retail security and loss prevention universe. Each issue is explained in a narrative format supplemented by diagrams, illustrations, and sample forms, as appropriate. Each chapter concludes with a checklist that highlights the significant points covered and can be used as a quick "refresher" on what you should remember. The checklists also provide an excellent reference source for conducting your own periodic in-store loss prevention analysis.

An overview of the issues covered in each Part of the book will give you a sampling of its value to you as a retail business owner or manager.

Part One   Personal Safety and Physical Security

Any meaningful discussion of loss prevention must begin by focusing on the protection of the most important assets of any retail establishment—you and your employees! If you and your staff cannot be safeguarded from loss of life, there will be no business. This part is designed to acquaint you with your most significant vulnerabilities and to provide you with practical guidance as to how you can best protect yourself and your employees. The following topics are covered:

- Proper opening and closing procedures
- After-hours precautions
- Bank deposit safeguards
- Civil unrest procedures
- Bomb threat guidelines
- Emergency kits

What actions must you take to safeguard the premises, building, and physical assets of your business? This most technical section of the book focuses on subjects such as locks, alarms, lighting, and closed-circuit television systems. Every attempt has been made to present this material in a simple, nontechnical manner, without using industry-specific jargon. Some standard, industrywide product descriptions are utilized. Your understanding of these data, plus a basic knowledge of product usage, will go a long way toward communicating with (and understanding) security-related business representatives regarding your physical security requirements.

- Selecting and properly securing doors and windows
- Choosing the right locks
- Effective key controls
- Alarm systems
- Lighting systems
- Fire, electrical, and water hazards.

Part Two   External Loss Prevention

This part pertains to the identification and prevention of losses inflicted on your business by external forces, that is, by nonemployees. Most people quickly identify the shoplifter as belonging in this category, but many others, of the same general ilk or worse, are just waiting for an opportunity to separate you from your money and your merchandise. Among them are armed robbers, burglars, bad-check passers, fraudulent credit card users, and a wide assortment of scam, fraud, and "con" artists. The only way you are going to be able to protect yourself from these criminals is to learn all you can about them. This material will help you to identify them, tell you how they operate, and give you some good information as to how you can protect your business from the losses they cause. The following topics are covered:

- Shoplifting
- Armed robbery
- Check fraud
- Credit card fraud
- Counterfeit currency

- Fast-change and confidence artists
- Vendor controls
- Exchange and refund fraud.

Part Three   Internal Loss Prevention

The focus of this part is the prevention of losses caused by your own employees. It is a sad but true fact that, unless you operate in a high-crime area and are subjected to frequent armed robberies and on-slaughts by professional shoplifting rings, you are in all likelihood going to suffer more losses as a consequence of the dishonest acts of your own employees than from all other sources put together. A very sobering thought. Fortunately, this is the one aspect of an effective loss prevention program where you can exercise the most control. The following topics are covered:

- Employee evaluations and relations
- Prehire screenings
- New employee briefings
- Factors contributing to employee dishonesty
- Identifying "high-risk" employees
- Employee theft
- Personnel controls
- Merchandise controls
- Warehousing, receiving, shipping, and transporting controls
- Monetary controls
- Operational controls
- Terminations and arrests.

Conclusion

The final chapter puts your whole loss prevention approach together. Emphasis is on developing a loss prevention atmosphere in your store, providing for the requisite security, and training your supervisory and staff personnel in loss prevention. The information provided is augmented by a directory of suppliers who can help you develop and maintain your program (see Appendix).

The key ingredient in successful loss prevention is you. Nothing is going to happen unless you take the initiative and *make* it happen. You must demonstrate by your actions, your example, and your dedication that improving the loss prevention posture of your store is something you feel strongly about and fully intend to accomplish.

PART ONE

Personal Safety and Physical Security

A retail business requires two basic elements: personnel to run it and a premises or structure from which the business can be conducted. Both are essential . . . and both must be protected. If personnel are harmed or constantly put at risk, there will be no one available to operate the store. If the building is insecure and the contents open to loss by burglary, vandalism, or other causes, there will be nothing left to sell. In either case, the business will fail.

This part focuses on the important subjects of personal safety and physical security. It begins with information relating to the protection of the most valuable assets of the store—you and your employees. It then continues right on through by providing helpful data regarding such premises protection subjects as the proper securing of doors and windows, lock and key controls, and alarm systems.

Most store owners and managers are very knowledgeable of their product lines and well versed in the principles of marketing. Unfortunately, many of them are unaware of their vulnerabilities and uninformed as to the basic security and loss prevention actions they can take to safeguard their lives and their businesses. Information presented in the following chapters should help to rectify any such shortcomings.

CHAPTER ONE

Personal Safety

Your personal safety is, by any realistic standard of measurement, your most important concern. Personal injury is a greater threat than the theft of merchandise or cash. Small business owners are especially at risk and must safeguard against store burglaries, armed robbery, and other crimes that threaten bodily harm to store personnel.

OPENING AND CLOSING PROCEDURES

Store owners and managers are most vulnerable to armed robbery and serious bodily harm when engaged in either opening or closing their stores. The following paragraphs offer some general guidelines:

- **Never open your store alone.**

  Think about what you are doing and keep alert. As you approach the store and before getting out of your car, look around. If possible, drive around back and look at the doors, windows, and walls for signs of forced entry. If any ladders or ropes are dangling from the roof, burglars may still be inside. If you're suspicious about anything, call the police.

Make arrangements with your early-arriving employees to ensure that someone remains in position to go for help if you are held up while opening the store. If you must open with only one other employee present, make sure that employee does not immediately come into the store with you but stays outside until you give an "all clear" signal. If someone is hiding in the store and waiting for you, the employee posted outside will be available to call the police if you do not return to the front of the store and give the prearranged "all clear" signal within a certain specified period of time.

- **If you have no alternative and must open by yourself, make every effort to have someone check on your safety.**

Work out reciprocal arrangements with neighboring store owners. Signal or call each other at designated times. If you are in an isolated area and there is no one else around, set up a procedure with your spouse or a friend, to call you at a certain time (if you have not already called) and to ask the police to check on you if you don't answer the phone.

Always lock the front door after you enter, and keep it locked except to admit employees or until it is time to open for your normal business hours. Check for signs of a burglary. Be careful; the burglar could still be in the store. If you notice obvious signs that a burglary has been committed or see things that look suspicious, get out of the store, relock the door, and call the police. Let them check the entire premises before you reenter.

- **Take extra precautions at closing time.**

Lock all store funds in a safe. Do not leave any money in office drawers or in cash registers. Cash register drawers should be left open to preclude thieves from breaking them apart to look for cash. Lock all rear, side, or other auxiliary doors, windows, and other openings.

- **Make a complete area-by-area check for "hide-ins."**

  Some thieves hide in a store at closing time, break out later with merchandise, and quickly leave the scene with the aid of an accomplice. Others stay in a store all night to surprise and hold up the unsuspecting store owner whom they have observed opening alone. Pay particular attention, during your area check, to rest rooms (open the doors to the stalls), back hallways, trash rooms, boiler rooms, basements, and areas under stairs and conveyor belts.

- **Leave some lights on in the store.**

  This helps police patrols and others passing by to see any movement inside the store. Pay particular attention to lights in the office, the area around the safe, and departments containing high-value merchandise. Just prior to leaving, test and set the burglar alarm, lock the door, and, if utilized, set a time lock that records unauthorized reentries into the store. Before this ritual, check for suspicious persons or activity in the area. If something doesn't seem right to you, do not hesitate to call the police.

- **Never close the store alone and never remain in the store alone after closing hours.**

  This advice is of utmost importance. Try to keep as many employees with you as possible. It is strongly recommended that, shortly before you close, you have an employee leave the store and watch the entire closing procedure from a discreet distance. This employee should have a portable phone or be aware of the location of the nearest telephone and should know the telephone number of your local police. He or she should be posted while you exit the store, lock up, and safely leave the area.

AFTER-HOURS PRECAUTIONS

Once you have closed the store for the day and gone home, do not lower your loss prevention and personal safety guard. Numerous activities and ruses engaged in by the criminal element make it imperative that you keep your wits about you at all times.

Calls Back

Store owners and managers frequently receive after-hours calls requesting that they return to the store. Most of these calls are legitimate and pertain to such occurrences as fires, break-ins, alarm soundings, and the like, but many are not. *It is therefore imperative that, before leaving your residence, you call the appropriate official department or agency and confirm that they indeed called you.* This will eliminate the danger of your going to the store in response to a ruse and being robbed or assaulted. If the named officials did not call you, report the matter immediately to your local police department. Pharmacists and others who operate businesses that carry merchandise required in emergency situations are especially vulnerable to ruses of this nature. If you are in this category, notify your local police department of the situation before going to the store, and ask to have a police officer meet you there.

Break-Ins

Unless you are exceptionally fortunate, sooner or later your store is going to be broken into. When it happens, you will in all likelihood be informed of the break-in by the police. After confirming that it was indeed the police who called you, proceed to the store but *do not enter unless the police are there to go in with you.* Actually, it is much safer to open the door for the police and let them check out the interior of the store before you yourself go in. If the police are not there when you arrive, go to the nearest phone *away from the store* and call them, advising them that you are now near the store and are waiting for their arrival.

If, in fact, a burglary has occurred and funds and merchandise are missing, or if serious damage has resulted, follow the instructions of the police. Do not touch or disturb anything of possible evidentiary value. In all cases, an itemized list of merchandise taken will be required by the police. Make extra copies for yourself, your insurance company, and other officials, as appropriate. The list should fully describe the items taken, the serial numbers (if known), the model numbers, the quantities taken, and the prices. Special notifications, which you should be aware of, must be made if items such as narcotics, weapons, explosives, or other dangerous chemicals or materials are stolen.

Occasionally, your store may be broken into during the night, possibly through the roof or a wall, in a way that avoids your burglar alarm. The burglary will not be detected until you open the store the following morning. *One of the first things you should do upon opening is to look for signs of a break-in.* Check the ceiling, the air shafts, and the perimeter walls. If any sign of a break-in is detected, immediately call your servicing police department.

Your primary purposes after a break-in are to keep people out, at the location of the illegal entry, and to protect the areas where money, merchandise, or sensitive materials may have been taken, disturbed, or strewn about. Get a rope from your emergency storage kit (described later in this chapter) and cordon off all appropriate areas. Instruct all employees not to go into or near any disturbed area until the police arrive and complete their investigation. Do not discuss the incident with anyone except the police and others who have an official reason to know details.

BANK DEPOSIT SAFEGUARDS

Ranking alongside your degree of vulnerability if you use improper opening and closing procedures is the risk inherent in the use of dangerous bank deposit procedures. All too often, store owners and managers allow this daily—and bank deposits should be made daily—procedure to become so routine and commonplace that it becomes an unthinking, almost subconscious activity. Receipts are gathered up, placed in clearly marked and obvious bank deposit bags and casually carried to a nearby bank. Such bad habits must be broken because they present an enormous risk to the person making the deposit. He or she becomes an easy and obvious target for a crime.

At the very least, vary the times you make your deposits and conceal the deposit bag. The bags provided by servicing banks are so obvious and so familiar to criminals that to be seen openly carrying one is tantamount to pleading, "Take me, take me!" Do not carry the deposit bag openly. Put it inside a store shopping bag, a purse, or a briefcase, or under a garment.

- **If at all possible, do not make the deposit by yourself.**

  Make every effort to be accompanied by another employee. The second individual should follow at a discreet distance. If you are held up, your companion can summon help. The same procedure should be followed when making night deposits, especially if they are made after closing the store for the night and even if you have to drive to your bank to make the deposit. Have someone follow you in another car and observe your activities until you have safely made the deposit and left the area. In addition to this individual's benefit to your personal safety, he or she could serve as a witness in case you are ever wrongfully accused of fabricating a holdup.

- **Be extremely alert when dropping off deposits at bank repository boxes.**

  Check the surrounding area carefully. If persons in the area look suspicious or things just don't seem right, leave the area immediately. If you are followed, go to a heavily populated, well-lighted area and call the police.

  Double-check all deposits made after normal banking hours, where you are required to use the night deposit box provided by the bank. Before relocking the box and leaving, always make certain that your deposit bag disappears into the repository and is not caught or snagged in the chute.

- **Consider using the services of an armored car company.**

  This is especially important if your business is located in a high-crime area or in a remote area that requires you to be away from your store for long periods of time in order to go to the bank. Keep in mind that your bank business frequently consists of two associated but distinctly separate and vulnerable functions. You go to the bank to make deposits but—and this is the point you shouldn't forget—you often bring back large amounts of change. Unfortunately, those heavily laden sacks of rolled coins can be deadly giveaways. Be careful! And reconsider the use of an armored car service.

- **Keep records of all bank deposits.**

  Banks are not infallible. Always retain a record, such as an adding machine tape, reflecting the composition of each bank deposit you make. Such records can be invaluable during investigations of claims made by banks that a deposit was "short." Keep your records with the daily cash reports to which they pertain. Whenever a deposit is made while the bank is open, request and retain the deposit slip validated by the bank teller who handles your deposit. Validated deposit slips for night deposits should be picked up on the next bank business day and verified against your records.

CIVIL UNREST PROCEDURES

There is no need to emphasize the dangers to retail businesses of riots and civil strife—recent history has made everyone painfully aware of them. Such outbreaks have occurred in the past and in all likelihood will occur in the future, with or without the usual accompanying violence. For your own personal safety and that of your employees and customers, you must stay attuned to current events occurring in the neighborhood of your store. Confrontations and disturbances can rapidly escalate to extremely dangerous levels, and you must know how to react. Stay tuned to local radio and television stations and to official channels of communication; keep abreast of crowd size, direction of movement, and mood. You may have to board up, evacuate, and close your store. Heed the advice of your local police department, and be aware of the following general guidelines:

- Business establishments that remain open or appear to be open during a disturbance do not suffer the same damage, looting, and fires as those establishments that close. Events, however, may require that you close for the safety of your customers and employees.

- If necessary, have people exit through a rear door.

- Keep with you as many employees as will voluntarily stay. Some may wish to remain because of a lack of safe exit or because they have no way to get home.

- Check all areas for unauthorized persons.

- Lock all outside doors, rest rooms, stock rooms, and trash rooms.

- Keep all lights on in the store.

- Have flashlights (and extra batteries) ready in case of power failure.

- Collect fire extinguishers and place them near doors and windows, in case fire bombs are thrown into the store.

- Connect garden hoses to faucets that have been adapted for their use.

- Assign someone to gather first-aid supplies and place them in a prearranged area.

- Empty all cash registers, leaving the drawers open, and lock the money in the safe. Include money order blanks and as much high-value merchandise as will fit.

- Have employees who remain appear to be working, but keep them away from doors and windows.

- Do not stand around inside or outside the store as if on "guard duty."

Incorporate as many of these recommendations as can be applied to your business into your formal company policies, and make them known to all employees.

BOMB THREAT GUIDELINES

When a person calls, or communicates in some other manner, to inform you that a bomb has been placed in your store, the caller usually wants to either avoid loss of life or create a disruption of business by causing an evacuation. Regardless of the fact that 95 to 99 percent of all bomb threats have proven to be hoaxes, they cannot be ignored. You must know and observe the following guidelines and go over them periodically with employees who are most likely to receive incoming calls. Setting forth this information on a card and posting it near the appropriate telephones is a good precautionary move (see Figure 1.1).

- If the threat is received by telephone, the individual taking the call should write down the exact time of the call. Record *exactly* what was said by the caller. Try to develop additional information. Can any background noises be heard? Laughter? Tinkling glasses? Loud conversations? Is the call possibly coming from inside the store? What about the voice? Is it familiar? Can you determine the sex of the caller? The approximate age? Is the speech slurred, or calm and rational? Do you detect any ethnic accent or unusual dialect?

- If possible, question the caller. Is he sure he has the right store? What is the correct location of the store? What kind of bomb is it? What does it look like? Where is it? Why was it placed? What time is it set to explode? If possible, keep the individual talking and try to alert someone else so the police can be notified and the call can possibly be traced.

FIGURE 1.1   Bomb Threat Info Form.

**BOMB THREAT
INFO CARD**

(Fold and place under or near telephone)

Date:_____Time:_____
Location:_____
Received By:_____
EXACT WORDING OF THREAT:
_____
_____
_____
_____
_____
_____
_____
_____

Length of Call:_____

CALLER ID:
Sex:_____   Age:_____

VOICE:
Familiar: Yes_____ No_____
Who sound like:_____

_____Normal   _____Soft/Loud
_____Excited   _____Laughing
_____Accent   _____Slurred
_____Rational   _____Angry
_____Clear   _____Vulgar
_____Other_____
_____

QUESTIONS TO ASK:

1. Sure you have right store?
2. Store location?
3. When is bomb to explode?
4. Where is it?
5. What does it look like?
6. What kind of bomb is it?
7. Did you place it?
8. Why?
9. What is your name?
10. Your address?
11. Where are you calling from?

BACKGROUND SOUNDS:

_____ Street noises?
_____Office noises?
_____Factory noises?
_____Animal noises?
_____Motors/Machinery?
_____Music?
_____Loud conversations?
_____Clear?
_____Static?
_____Coming from in store?
_____Other?_____

RECENT SIGNIFICANT INCIDENTS:
_____
_____

EVACUATE IF NECESSARY
————
NOTIFY ADJOINING
BUSINESSES

REPORT IMMEDIATELY TO:
Police:_____
Fire Dept:_____
Bomb Unit:_____

(Source: ProTect)

- If the threat is received by mail or through some other written communication, keep the handling of it to a minimum.
- Call your local police and fire departments.
- If a decision is made to evacuate the store, **avoid panic**. *Never* tell your customers they have to leave because there is a bomb in the store. Use a subterfuge; for example, go to your light panel and turn out all the lights for a few seconds. Repeat this a few times, gradually increasing the length of time the lights are off. You can then announce with some degree of credibility that you are experiencing electrical difficulties and that it will be necessary to turn off all the electrical power and evacuate the store.
- Unless you are the sole occupant of a stand-alone building, alert the owners and managers of adjoining businesses.
- If a detonation time has been given, clear the premises 15 to 30 minutes before the stated time and keep the store closed until approval for reopening has been given by local authorities.
- As in all cases of emergency evacuation, assign a responsible employee to check the rest rooms, basement, and stockroom areas for customers and employees who may be unaware of the danger. Lock all office funds in the safe. If time permits, collect the cash register receipts and lock them in the safe; if not, instruct employees to lock their registers and give you the keys. All employees should evacuate the store and gather at a place designated by you so you can ensure that they are all accounted for.
- A search of the premises will usually be made by the police. Employees, however, because of their knowledge of their work areas, have proven to be excellent resources when searching for unusual objects. The assistance of employees in such searches must be strictly voluntary. In addition, these volunteers must be told not to touch, move, or vibrate anything.
- If a bomb or any unusual object is found, point it out to the police and clear the area immediately.
- If no bomb is found, do not assume that there is none planted. Most bombs today do not look like bombs at all. They can be

disguised or hidden in cans, boxes, shopping bags, briefcases, or any number of common containers.

- Instruct your employees not to mention the reason for the evacuation to anyone and not to discuss the incident.

- As an aid to the investigation, try to recall whether you or anyone else in the store had any recent experience with any customer or employee that could have caused sufficient animosity to have prompted the bomb threat. If so, inform the police.

EMERGENCY KITS

Every store should maintain a well-stocked emergency kit. The contents of such kits are invaluable for protecting the building and the assets of the store in the event of civil disturbances, but they are also extremely useful in other emergencies such as fires, floods, power outages, break-ins, broken windows, and injuries. The kit should contain:

- First-aid supplies. An employee trained in CPR and emergency first-aid is a definite asset.

- Flashlights and fresh batteries, stored separately to prevent corrosion. In addition, flashlights should always be available in offices, in all department areas, and in rear work areas.

- Rope or clothesline of sufficient length to cordon off the area and prevent entry into the store.

- A quantity of "No Entry" and "No Trespassing" signs that can be posted on doors and walls and tied to cordons.

- Garden hoses fitted with spray nozzles and faucet adapters and of sufficient length to reach all portions of the store.

- An assortment of hardware items such as a hammer, nails, screwdrivers, pliers, duct tape, markers, knives, and scissors.

PERSONAL SAFETY CHECKLIST

Opening Procedures

☐ Check the store perimeter and surrounding area for suspicious signs.

☐ Make sure you have a backup when opening the store—never open the store alone.

☐ Develop an alerting procedure so someone can check on your safety.

☐ After opening, relock the door until your normal business hours.

Closing Procedures

☐ Lock all store funds in a safe.

☐ Empty all cash registers and leave them open.

☐ Lock and set the alarms for all rear, side, or auxiliary doors, windows, and other openings.

☐ Make a complete area-by-area check for "hide-ins."

☐ Make sure you leave the store sufficiently lighted.

☐ Test and set the burglar alarm.

☐ Before exiting, check the area for suspicious persons or activity.

☐ Never close the store alone.

☐ Make sure no one remains in the store after closing.

After-Hours Precautions

☐ Verify all calls requesting your return to the store.

☐ Notify the police and ask them to meet you at the store if you must return to handle a legitimate emergency.

(Continued)

(Continued)

☐ If you and/or members of your staff must remain in the store after normal closing hours, ensure that all exterior doors are locked and notify your local police and alarm company.

Break-Ins

☐ Check for signs of unlawful entry before opening the store.

☐ If such signs are noted, prohibit everyone from entering the store until the police arrive and make a thorough check of the premises.

☐ Check for signs of a burglary immediately after opening the store.

☐ If a burglary has occurred, make sure the area is protected and don't touch anything until the police arrive and complete their investigation.

☐ Inform all employees that they are not to discuss any break-ins with anyone except the police and others who have official reasons to know details.

☐ Make an accurate list, as soon as possible, of all merchandise taken. Make copies of the list for the police and the insurance company.

Bank Deposit Safeguards

☐ Vary the time you make deposits.

☐ Make every effort to have someone escort or shadow the individual making the deposit.

☐ Conceal easily identifiable bank bags on the way to the bank.

☐ Check the area around bank deposit boxes for suspicious activity before approaching, especially at night.

(Continued)

☐ Double-check that deposits placed in night-deposit boxes do not get caught or snagged in the chute.

☐ Keep a record reflecting the composition of each deposit.

Civil Unrest Procedures

☐ Monitor current events and potentially disruptive activities occurring in the neighborhood of the store.

☐ Develop civil unrest policies and inform all employees.

☐ As applicable, follow all recommended procedures described earlier in the chapter.

Bomb Threat Guidelines

☐ Treat seriously all bomb threats.

☐ Train all employees, especially those who respond to incoming telephone calls, to handle bomb threats.

☐ Keep Bomb Threat Info Forms (see Figure 1.1) near every telephone.

☐ Make sure all supervisory and staff employees are knowledgeable regarding proper store evacuation procedures.

Emergency Kits

☐ Maintain a well-stocked emergency kit.

☐ Make sure someone on the staff is trained in emergency first-aid procedures.

CHAPTER TWO

Physical Security

A fter you have taken steps to safeguard your personal safety, what must you do to ensure that there is still a business establishment for you to manage? *Physical security* refers to actions taken to safeguard the building, the premises, and the physical assets of a business. Space limitations make it impossible to provide detailed data regarding every type of retail establishment. The information provided in this chapter is applicable to most of them.*

Doors, windows, and other openings to the premises comprise the first set of vulnerabilities leading to unauthorized entry into your store. An understanding of their structures, installations, locking mechanisms, and alarm devices is essential to the establishment of a successful physical security program. Knowledge and application of the principles involved constitute your first line of defense. The various

* *Special Note:* Depictions of security products presented in this book are for illustrative purposes only and do not constitute endorsement by the author or the publisher. Your best source of on-the-scene information is the professional, licensed locksmiths and security device installation firms servicing your area.

types of doors and windows and their methods of installation will be addressed first. Additional discussions will inform you on locks and alarms.

First, let's take a look at the various means burglars use to break in. The average burglar is, first of all, an opportunist—always looking, literally, for that "window (or door) of opportunity." Burglars make a practice of testing all doors and windows to see whether any have been left unlocked or unsecured and might allow easy entry. If unsuccessful, burglars move on to the next stage—the use of force. They can gain entry through brute force or by using the most basic tools in a variety of ways. Burglars can gain entry in any of the following ways:

- **Kicking.** A few hard kicks in the vicinity of the lockset will open many doors. What usually happens is that the door frame breaks away or the screws holding the strike plate to the frame pop loose. Some burglars don't even bother with trying to kick open the lock; instead, they concentrate on kicking out the panels of the door itself, particularly if the door is thin and poorly constructed.

- **Shimmying.** This method is used almost exclusively to defeat locks that consist of only a latch bolt, that is, the type of locking mechanism that is beveled and will retract under pressure. All a burglar has to do is slide a *shim,* a thin piece of metal or plastic, between the lock and the frame, and the door can be easily opened.

- **Jimmying.** A screwdriver, a prybar, or even a tire iron is all that a burglar needs to force open or "jimmy" a lock. Such tools are usually used on doors that do not fit well in their frames and are equipped with locks that have short latch or dead bolts. The tool is forced between the door and the frame, and leverage is applied to separate the locking bolt from the frame.

- **Sawing.** The next step up from jimmying, this method, which employs the use of a hacksaw blade, is used to defeat locks that, although they may be mounted on ill-fitting doors, use longer dead bolts that prevent jimmying. The hacksaw is used to cut through the dead bolt or cut into it far enough so that it will yield to kicking.

- **Pounding, prying, and pulling.** This is really the use of brute force. The lock, and often the door itself and the hinges, are attacked with a variety of tools—sledgehammers, pipewrenches, heavy pieces of metal, cinder blocks, or large stones. You name it and if it is handy and can serve the purpose, a burglar intent on entry will use it.

- **Drilling.** We're now moving away from the "common" burglar and into the realm of the professional. This is especially so when the lock that is drilled out, with the aid of sophisticated tools, is affixed to a safe or vault. Drilling out a lock on a perimeter door is a snap for most professional burglars. Unfortunately, the field is expanding and includes many semiprofessionals who use the wide variety of cordless electric drills now on the market to drill out locks and gain entry.

- **Picking.** In this method, the burglar, usually a professional, uses a set of thin metal rods with hooks on the ends of them. The rod is inserted into the keyway as a key substitute, and is then manipulated and turned so as to align the pins in the lock cylinder. Once the pins are aligned, the locking mechanism can be turned, thereby moving and retracting the latch or dead bolt and opening the door.

Now that we know how burglars get in, let's take a look at your vulnerabilities and see what can be done to correct them.

DOORS

Poorly constructed, inappropriate, ill-fitting, and improperly installed exterior doors make it relatively simple for burglars to enter your store. A close examination of the doors you have and some simple precautions and modifications can put the odds back in your favor. First, take a look at the door frames. Even the heaviest of steel doors are worthless if they are attached to weak, split, or rotted wooden frames. Repair or replace them immediately if you note such conditions, preferably using metal frames.

Next, examine the hinges that secure the door to the frame. Can you see them with the door closed? If you can, and they are on the outside, as they are in many old buildings, you may have a problem. There is no need for a burglar to pick your lock or cut holes into the door panels to gain entry, if all he has to do is remove the screws holding the door to the frame and lift off the entire door in one easy operation. Have the door rehung so that the hinges are not visible, at least, replace the old slotted screws with one-way, nonretractable screws as soon as possible. While you are at it, replace the hinges with new hinges that have nonremovable pins. You'll thwart an easy tapping out of the hinge pin and removal of the door in that manner. To be really secure, have the entire assembly welded to the door and to the frame.

Doors are vulnerable not only through their frame, hinges, and lock assemblies but also through structural deficiencies and inappropriate use. Unfortunately, many hollow-core and lightweight wood-paneled doors designed for interior use are improperly installed in exterior, point-of-entry doorways. Primary doors should be of metal or solid-core wood construction at least 2 inches thick, without panels and with a good, tight flush fit to the door frame.

Don't concentrate all your attention on your front door; your rear and side doors are more likely to be challenged by burglars because such doors are usually located where burglars can work unobserved. If you are in a multistoried building, don't forget about your upper-level fire exit doors. Can they be reached from the ground via pull-down ladders?

Simple supplemental devices that are especially suitable for rear and side doors can be utilized to provide additional break-in protection. One of the most common devices is a bolting mechanism that is either surface-mounted or internally mounted on a door, with the bolt extending into the frame. Metal bars or sturdy wooden bars can also be installed on the interior of doors, with the bars extending beyond the frames. In addition, steel pins and bolts may be installed on the sides and tops of doors that have corresponding holes in the door frames, to prevent the doors from being pried off or lifted out of their frames. An example of a high-security door with a multilocking mechanism is shown in Figure 2.1.

Although these safeguards pertain, for the most part, to preventing entry when the store is closed, some doors must also be protected during business hours. In most situations of this type, owners rely on appropriate alarm systems, but, as will be discussed later, other actions may be necessary. For example, if rear doors must be open for ventilation purposes, it may be necessary to install an additional door constructed of metal bars or heavy screening and secured from the inside by a key or other locking mechanism. The use of peepholes, door chains, and door guards, which allow a door to be opened only 2 inches, may also be appropriate. Are you sure that the man ringing the bell at your rear receiving door is really a delivery man? Take a look and check him out before you fully open your door and let him into your store.

Every store should have only one primary point-of-entry and, because it is usually the most visible, it should be the front door. The keyways of all other exterior doors should be plugged or in some manner rendered inoperative and set up so that they can be opened only from the inside. This procedure will not only make it more difficult for burglars to gain entry but, more importantly, it will prevent after-hours reentry into the store by dishonest employees who have access to or who have made duplicate keys.

WINDOWS

Windows present problems of a different nature. Unless you want your store to look like a fortress, you will have large expanses of windows, both for display purposes and to create a bright, pleasant shopping atmosphere. Even when a window has an alarm, it doesn't take long for a thief to throw a trash can through the glass, climb into the store, grab merchandise, exit, and be gone before the police arrive. Other than resorting to the use of metal roll-down protective covers

FIGURE 2.1   Door with Four-Point Locking Mechanism.

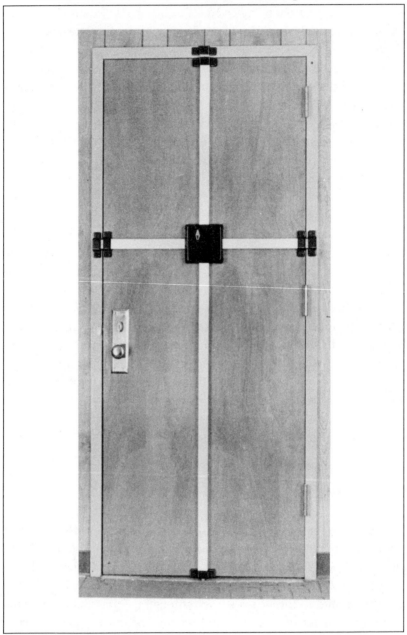

(*Source:* SECURITECH Group, Inc.)

and scissors-type grills that are almost mandatory in high-crime areas and during periods of civil unrest, there isn't much you can do to minimize such illegal entries other than keeping the interior area well lighted.

You can, however, do something about other windows in the store. Unless they must be opened periodically, all windows in the store, especially those that cannot be seen from the office or main sales floor, should be permanently closed. Bolt them to the frame with lag bolts with the heads recessed, to prevent their being removed as a unit. Then protect them with ½-inch round steel bars secured in the masonry at least 3 inches. Follow that by covering the entire assembly with heavy wire mesh. You are striving here to create a defensive situation that will not only prevent burglars from crawling in but will keep shoplifters and dishonest employees from throwing merchandise out, especially through windows located in rest rooms, back hallways, and stockrooms.

If you have windows that must occasionally be opened, keep them secured with the type of sliding bolt lock that uses a combination padlock as the locking mechanism. Keep the combination confidential, known only to store management.

OTHER OPENINGS

Frequently overlooked in the perimeter protection planning process is the identification and safeguarding of miscellaneous openings in your store—ventilation shafts, air ducts, skylights, and trap doors—that allow for surreptitious entry. The protection methodology for such openings usually consists of both locks and alarms, with emphasis on the latter. They are mentioned here, rather than in the section devoted to alarm devices, in order to provide you with a better understanding of your total perimeter vulnerabilities.

- **Ventilation shafts and air ducts.** Many burglars use shafts and ducts to enter stores, especially when access to the shafts is from the roof. It really is a simple matter to remove a shaft cover or duct hood, secure a rope (or have a partner hold it), and drop or crawl down into the store.

These openings must be protected. If at all possible, do it from the roof or shaft origination end. Use heavy-gauge wire mesh or steel bars welded or bolted to the frame or roof with nonretractable bolts. In the same manner, secure any shaft terminus that allows entry into your store. As an added measure, such openings should be incorporated into your store burglar alarm system. Your alarm installer will utilize a wire grid method called "trapping" to protect such areas.

- **Skylights.** Skylights are an even easier means to enter your store. Protect them in the same way.

- **Trap doors.** In most buildings, any number of small doors provide access to the roof. Such doors must be locked and alarmed.

- **Common walls.** The common walls referred to here are those separating your business from those of your adjoining business neighbors. It may seem odd to be discussing common walls in a section captioned "Other Openings." However, all too often, common walls abutting neighboring businesses are overlooked or not closely examined. If your business is located in a strip mall or a building that has had a lot of tenant movement and renovation, pay particular attention to your common walls and the crawl space above your ceilings. Frequently, you will find that what you assumed to be a common firewall extending to the roof line is a partial wall that extends only a short distance above the ceiling. This type of construction gives an open invitation to burglars. They can easily remove or slide open a ceiling panel on one side of the wall, crawl up and over, and come down on the other side— right into your store. This vulnerability is particularly exploitable by dishonest employees of adjacent businesses, especially if entry can be gained from rear storage areas and can provide access to your stockrooms. Many merchants have lost thousands of dollars' worth of merchandise to such "ghost thefts" and never knew why. Don't let it happen to you!

Most "short walls" are noted by local fire marshals, but many are not. If you have a short-wall problem, get together with your business neighbors and correct it. If a wall cannot be properly extended to the roof line, try to have some heavy metal bars or heavy-gauge wire screening installed. At the very least, bring it to the attention of your alarm installer so that the area can be "trapped" with contacts and a grid of alarmed wires and properly safeguarded.

LOCKS AND KEYS

Once the right type of door is selected and then properly installed, the next line of defense is the locks. Where should they be installed and what type should be used?

The first part of that question is easy to answer. All perimeter doors that allow access into the store should be protected by locks. Recommending a specific type of lock, however, becomes a bit more difficult. Gone are the days when locks were just a padlock or some sort of key-operated handle or knob mechanism. Locks now range from relatively simple combination or push-button devices to complex electromagnetic systems operated by a variety of coded card readers and remote signals. There are even locks that operate on a voice-recognition signal, and others, used to protect extremely sensitive areas, that are activated by precoded thumbprints or palm prints. In short, you have a wide variety of locks from which to choose. Selecting the types that are best suited for your location, your line of merchandise, and your budget can best be done with the assistance of a competent, licensed locksmith. A list of lock companies is provided in the Appendix.

To be able to discuss your needs with your locksmith, you should know something about the more common locking devices available and the primary uses for which they are intended. Such knowledge will also help you to better understand and evaluate the locksmith's recommendations. Keep in mind that your locksmith is not a mind reader. If you carry security-sensitive or high-value merchandise, have unusual store layouts, or conduct business activities that impact on your lock requirements, tell him. He is, after all, a bit like a doctor—he can't provide the cure unless you can describe all the symptoms. Remember to comply with all of your local building code requirements, especially those affecting the functions of locks used on fire doors and emergency exit doors.

Types of Locks

Without getting too technical, let's take a look at the world of locks. To make sense of this section, you'll need the following definitions.

- **Latch bolt.** The angled or beveled end of the lock mechanism that projects from the front of the lock. When the door is swung shut, the extended latch bolt slides into a hole in a metal plate (the strike) affixed to the door frame. The locking mechanism can be configured to work by simply turning the door knob, or by using a key or a thumb latch. This is the most common type of locking mechanism. It is used most frequently on locks for interior doors leading to closets, bedrooms, and bathrooms. It is also

FIGURE 2.2 Typical Latch Bolt Lock.

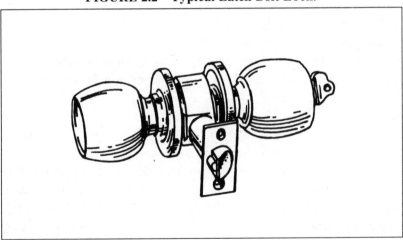

(*Source:* Safemasters, Inc.)

the most insecure of locking devices: it can easily be defeated by sliding a shim, such as a thin piece of metal or a credit card, between the door and the frame and against the beveled latch. When used on an entry door, a latch bolt must be backed up with another type of lock that will provide much better protection. (See Figure 2.2 for a sketch of a latch bolt.)

- **Dead bolt.** The part of the locking mechanism that protrudes from the lock body. When extended (thrown), it fits into a hole cut into a metal plate (strike) attached to the door frame. The primary feature of the dead bolt is that, unlike the latch bolt, when it is in the closed (locked) position, the bolt will not retract with end pressure. The use of the dead bolt is strongly recommended for all store perimeter doors, stockrooms, offices, and other areas where a high degree of protection is necessary. Locks using the dead bolt principle are made for a wide variety of

FIGURE 2.3   Cylindrical Dead Bolt Lock.

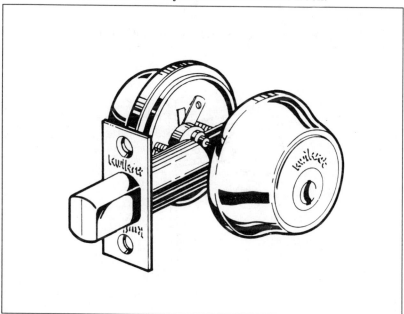

(*Source:* Kwikset, Corp.)

purposes and come in many styles and configurations. Some examples are shown in Figures 2.3, 2.4, and 2.5.

- **Cylinder.** The subassembly of the lock, which contains the locking mechanism. (See Figure 2.6.)

- **Core.** That portion of the lock assembly containing only the keying plug and the tumbler mechanism. The cores of many locks are removable for easy replacement, an extremely desirable feature. (See Figure 2.7 for a sketch of a core assembly.)

- **Tumbler (pin tumbler).** The part of the locking mechanism that is contained within the core. It consists of a number (the more the better) of short, spring-activated rods, commonly referred to as pins or tumblers. When the pins are properly aligned by the turn of a matching key, the mechanism becomes operational and the latching device, such as a dead bolt, is then extended to lock the

FIGURE 2.4   Mortise Dead Bolt Lock.

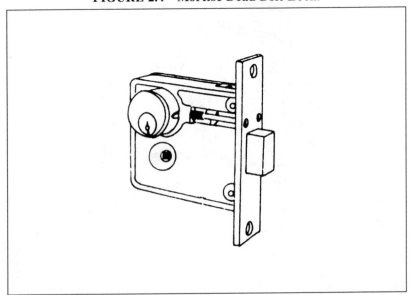

(*Source:* Safemasters, Inc.)

FIGURE 2.5 Dual Latch Bolt and Dead Bolt Lock.

(*Source:* Arrow Lock Mfg. Co.)

FIGURE 2.6   Cylinder Assembly.

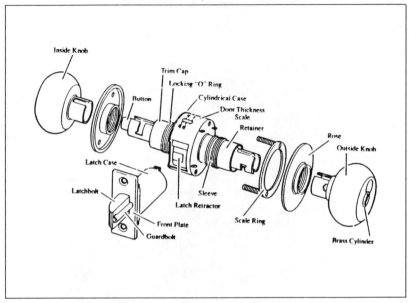

(*Source:* Medeco Security Locks)

door or retracted to unlock it. (See Figure 2.8 for an exploded view of a pin tumbler assembly.)

- **Strike.** A metal plate fastened to a door frame; a bolt or latch projects into the strike.

- **Strike box.** The housing, including the space in back of the strike, that is used to enclose and protect the bolt and the bolt opening. Strike assemblies should be mounted with long (at least 2½- or 3-inch) screws. (See Figure 2.9 for a diagram of a strike assembly.)

- **Cylindrical lockset.** The most common type of door lock. It consists of a locking mechanism enclosed within a cylindrical chamber and mounted to a door through a large bored hole. It usually has a knob or handle on each side of the door. (See Figure 2.10 for an example of this type of lockset.)

FIGURE 2.7 Lock Core.

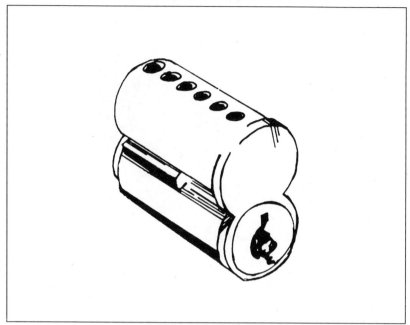

(*Source:* Safemasters, Inc.)

- **Mortise lockset.** A type of locking mechanism, usually rectangular, that is mounted within the outside edge of a door frame (the stile). Most glass and narrow metal framed store doors utilize mortise locksets. In addition to having door knobs activating a latch bolt assembly for open-hours convenience, the better mechanisms, as depicted in Figure 2.5, also incorporate a separate key-operated dead bolt lock. (See Figure 2.11 for an example of this type of lockset.)

- **Auxiliary and specialty locksets.** A generic description of secondary locks, usually of the dead bolt variety, that are used to reinforce the primary lock. The term is also used to describe locks that, although they may operate on the latch bolt or dead bolt principle, use different activating mechanisms and are often

FIGURE 2.8   Pin Tumbler Assembly.

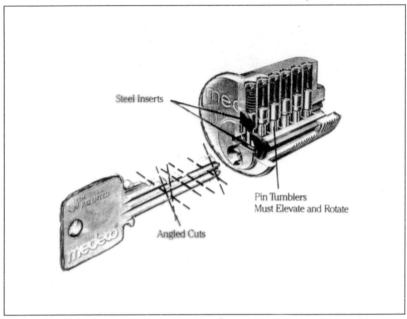

Steel Inserts

Pin Tumblers
Must Elevate and Rotate

Angled Cuts

(*Source:* Medeco Security Locks)

designed for specific and unique purposes. Included in this category are: locks that operate by push buttons, magnetic card readers, and a wide variety of remote control electromagnetic and
electromechanical release devices, and several different types of
dead bolt locks that mount on exterior doors. Locking devices for
fire doors and emergency exit doors are also in this group, but,
because of their specialized nature, they will be discussed later in
this chapter. (For examples of the wide variety of auxiliary and
specialty locks available, see Figures 2.12 through 2.15.)

Choosing Locks

Unless you are located in a very modern building with advanced security controls, your doors, particularly at your point-of-entry, are most
likely going to be of the mortise type and key-operated (refer back to

FIGURE 2.9   Strike Assembly.

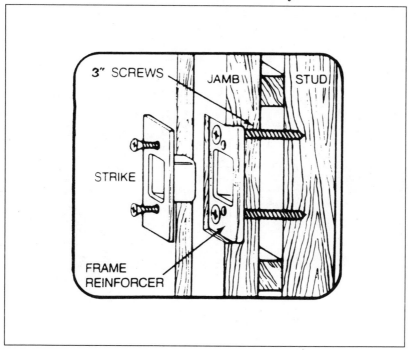

(*Source:* Schlage Lock Co.)

FIGURE 2.10   Cylindrical Lockset.

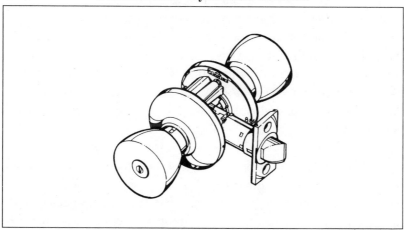

(*Source:* Master Lock Co.)

FIGURE 2.11   Mortise Lockset.

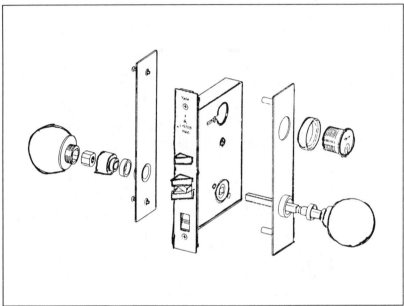

(*Source:* Yale Security Inc.)

Figure 2.4). Depending on your business environment, you may choose to use a locking device that is activated by a magnetic card reader or a combination push button. Regardless of the type of operating mechanism, insist that the lock have a dead bolt with at least a 2-inch extension (the sliding part of the lock that goes into the frame or stile). If the primary lock does not have a dead bolt, install a second, auxiliary lock that does. You undoubtedly have an additional lock installed at your residence. (If you don't, you should.) Provide the same protection for your business.

If possible, insist that the locks are of the pin tumbler type, with at least five pins, and that the core cylinder is easily removable and interchangeable. In the event you feel the key to the lock has been compromised—that is, someone has had improper access to it or may have had it copied—you can immediately change the locking mechanism

FIGURE 2.12   Push-Button-Operated Locks.

(*Source:* Simplex Access Security Controls—Division of ILCO/UNICAN Corp.)

FIGURE 2.13   Electromagnetic Locks.

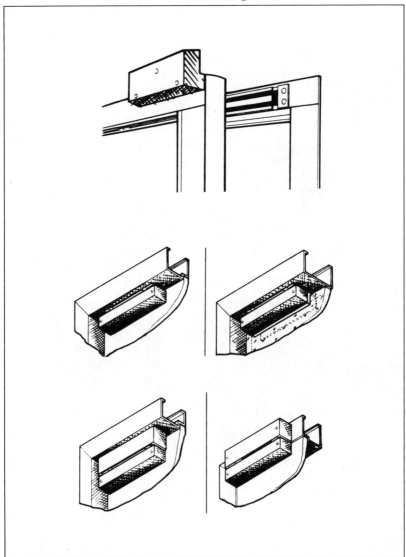

(*Source:* LOCKNETICS Security Engineering)

FIGURE 2.14   Electromechanical Locks.

(*Source:* LOCKNETICS Security Engineering)

and the key by switching the core with a spare set kept on hand in your safe.

As previously mentioned, all perimeter doors other than the one point-of-entry door should be made inoperable from the outside. In addition to their being alarmed and secured with a variety of bolts, bars, and chains, these doors also need to be locked. Strong, key-operated dead bolts are preferable, but padlocks are used in many such situations.

FIGURE 2.15 Surface Mounted Bolt Locks.

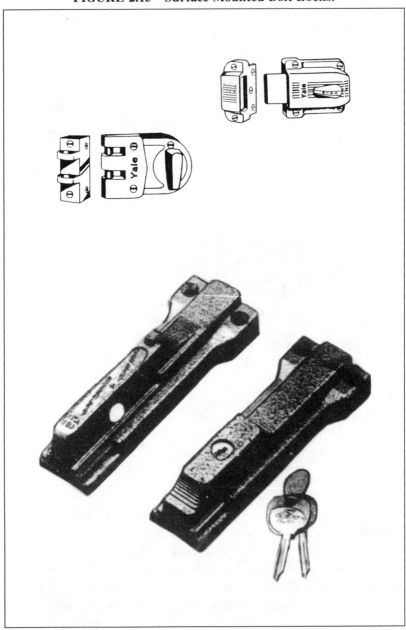

(*Source:* Yale Security Inc. (top) and Sargent & Greenleaf, Inc. (bottom))

Padlocks

Padlocks, as locking devices, are in a class by themselves. Their varieties and purposes are almost endless. They range from the very simple, easily picked types to the most complex of combination, special keyed, and shielded varieties. If you must use a padlock, get a sturdy one that operates with a pin tumbler mechanism. The case and the shackle should be made of hardened steel. For extra protection, consider using a sturdy, high-security combination padlock. (See Figures 2.16 and 2.17 for examples of the variety of padlocks available.)

Padlocks have one major drawback: they must be mounted on something—a hasp. The strongest padlock in the world is worthless if it is mounted on a hasp that can easily be pulled apart or pried away from its fasteners. A strong mounting hasp, properly secured, is an absolute must when using padlocks. Get one that comes with a hinged locking bar that, when in place, conceals the mounting screws (see Figure 2.18). If a door or area protected by a padlock is to remain open for

FIGURE 2.16   General Purpose Padlocks.

(*Source:* Master Lock Co.)

FIGURE 2.17   High Security Padlocks.

(*Source:* Master Lock Co.)

any length of time, relock the padlock on the mounting hasp. This will prevent anyone from switching the lock and reentering later for purposes of theft.

Fire Doors and Emergency Exits

Special attention must be given to locking devices installed on doors designated as fire or emergency exits. This subject will be addressed in detail when we discuss alarms, but some general warnings are in order here.

Scrupulously obey all fire regulations and building codes relating to fire doors and emergency exit doors. Equally important, see to it that your employees obey them. *Do not chain, bolt, padlock, or otherwise affix any type of device to one of these doors, to hinder it from quickly opening from the inside in the event of an emergency.* Do not block the

FIGURE 2.18   Hasps with Hinged Locking Bars.

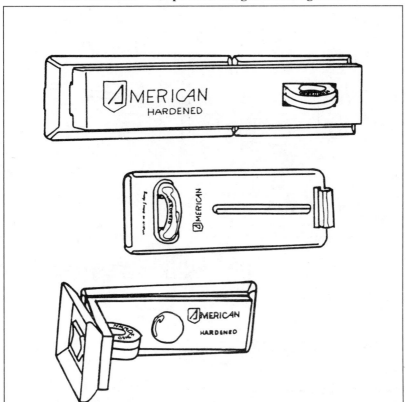

(*Source:* American Lock Co.)

door by stacking merchandise, trash, or other materials in front of it. Be sure the hallways leading to the doors are clear.

By law, all emergency doors must be equipped on the interior side with some type of broad panic bar or paddle which, when pressed or pushed against, immediately opens the door. When necessary, the exterior of the door can be equipped with a keyway to operate the locking mechanism. (See Figure 2.19 for examples of emergency exit devices.)

FIGURE 2.19   Emergency Exit Devices.

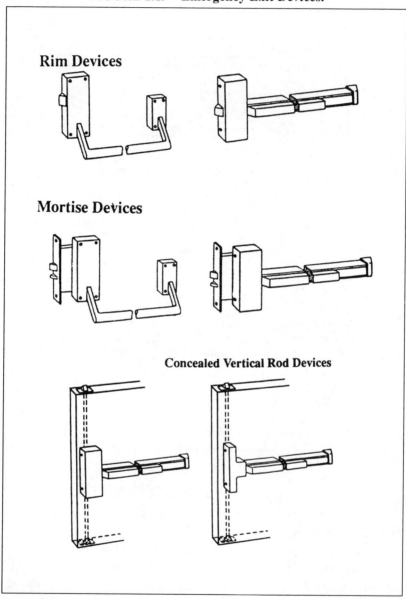

(*Source:* Safemasters, Inc.)

OTHER LOCKED AREAS

In addition to perimeter doors, other areas that should be secured by locks include offices, stockrooms, and, where possible, rest rooms. Cash drawers and cabinets containing security-sensitive or high-value merchandise should also be locked. Figure 2.20 shows examples of drawer and cabinet locks. Showcase locks to secure sliding glass door display cases are also available (see Figure 2.21).

TIME LOCKS

Before concluding this discussion of locks, one more type must be mentioned—the time lock. The time lock referred to here is different from the type commonly associated with bank vaults and safes. Its purpose is to prevent internal theft by employees—more specifically, by management employees. If the nature or size of your business requires that you have various shifts or must rely on someone else to open or close the store, you have a potential problem. Unless you use a card-reader locking system that automatically monitors and records each time a door is opened, or have contracted with a central station alarm system that will notify you of every instance when the burglar alarm is turned off during periods when the store is closed, *you are vulnerable to unauthorized reentry and theft of merchandise by dishonest managers and assistant managers.* If you have no alarm system at all, you are really courting disaster. *You need a time lock!*

A time lock is a secondary device that must be unlocked to gain entry into the store. Only you should have the key. Attached to the point-of-entry door, the time lock will provide you with a written record of all after-hours entries. Mere installation of such a lock acts as a powerful deterrent to any "biting-the-hand-that-feeds-you" actions.

KEY CONTROL

As practical and as sturdy as they may be, *key-operated locks have one major drawback—they are only as good as the control exercised over*

FIGURE 2.20   Drawer and Cabinet Locks.

Drawer/Door Cam Locks   **Drawer Spring Bolt Locks**

Drawer Dead Bolt Locks   **Drawer/Door Spring Bolt Locks**

(*Source:* Kenstan Lock Co.)

FIGURE 2.21   Sliding Door Locks.

Sliding Door Ratchet Locks

Sliding Door Plunger Locks

(*Source:* Kenstan Lock Co.)

the keys that open them. Because of this vulnerability, certain keys should be exclusively retained and controlled by store management. They are: the keys to the locks on front and rear entry doors, high-value stockrooms, the manager's office, and, for larger, multiunit businesses, company stock delivery trucks.

Every store should have a key plan. All major lock companies manufacture locks that can be keyed for different degrees or levels of access:

- **The grand master key.** The owner's or manager's key. It can open all lock groups that have been keyed to work with it.

- **The master key.** The department manager's key. It can open all lock groups within one specific department or area that have been keyed to work with it.

- **The individual key.** The general employee's key. It will open only one lock, or perhaps a series of cabinets or showcase locks, located within the employee's immediate work area.

Many lock manufacturers make key-operated locks that allow the key to be removed only when the lock is in the secure or locked position. These locks, referred to as "captive" locks, are excellent choices for cash drawers. Most cash register and point-of-sale terminals utilize such locks. Having the key in the lock is a graphic reminder to the responsible employee that the drawer can be opened.

A number of lock companies make high-security keyed locks with unique keying mechanisms that can only be operated by keys that have been precisely and specially cut. Duplicate or replacement keys for such locks cannot be made by standard key-cutting machines. They must be ordered from the factory, where the lock and its owner are registered and strict accountability is maintained.

If key loss or replacement is a problem, you should seriously consider one of the many combination, push-button, cypher, or card reader locks that are currently available. These locks eliminate the aggravation and worry of lost or stolen keys. Equally significant, they allow you to quickly and frequently change their operating codes, a desirable and strongly recommended practice.

Even if you don't need to resort to such a high level of security, there are a number of other key control practices that you should follow:

- **Limit the number of keys issued.**

- **Number the keys.** To instill in your employees a sense of responsibility for key care, number each key issued. Simple-to-use metal stamping kits are available at most hardware stores. Require each employee to sign a receipt for each key received.

- **Maintain a log of keys issued.** At the very least, the log should reflect the date of issue; the name of the individual receiving the key; the location of the door or cabinet for which the key was issued; and the key number. The log should also have a space to note whether the key was returned when the employee was transferred, resigned, or terminated.

- **Stamp "Do Not Duplicate" on all keys issued.**

- **Do not tag keys with the store name or with any address.**

- **Conduct periodic (at least quarterly) inventories of all keys issued.**

- **Rekey locks periodically under normal conditions.** Rekey immediately at the time of departure of supervisory personnel and when other employees leave under less than favorable circumstances.

- **Keep unissued and spare keys in a safe to which only you have the combination, or in a separate, locked cabinet.** A number of good key cabinets are available. Some, in addition to being very secure and fireproof, contain automated access, monitoring, and dispensing devices. An example of such a system is shown in Figure 2.22. Other key control systems are depicted in Figure 2.23.

Salespersons must be instructed in proper key control procedures. Cash register keys must be pulled out and retained by the person responsible, when duties take him or her away from the immediate vicinity of the register. The key should not be put into another register drawer, on a shelf or a hook, or in some box beneath or behind the counter. Such actions, which only have to be observed once, leave the register wide open to thieves. They can strike when they next find the register area unattended or, as frequently happens, they can clean out the register after causing the clerk to check a back stockroom for an item in which they profess interest.

The keys to showcase locks also require special handling. They should be kept in the register drawer of the salesperson on duty. At closing time, they should be turned in with the day's receipts and locked in the safe. These actions will prevent the keys from being found and used when the department is not staffed or during a break-in.

Managers should carry only those keys necessary for the daily operation of the store. Infrequently used, excess, or duplicate keys should be tagged and left in a safe or in a secure key cabinet. Do not carry all of your keys on one ring. Divide them into two groups, an exterior group (perimeter doors, time lock, bank deposit box, and so on) and an interior group (stockrooms, register reading keys, day alarms, and so on). This practice will deny dishonest employees any

FIGURE 2.22   Security Key Monitor.

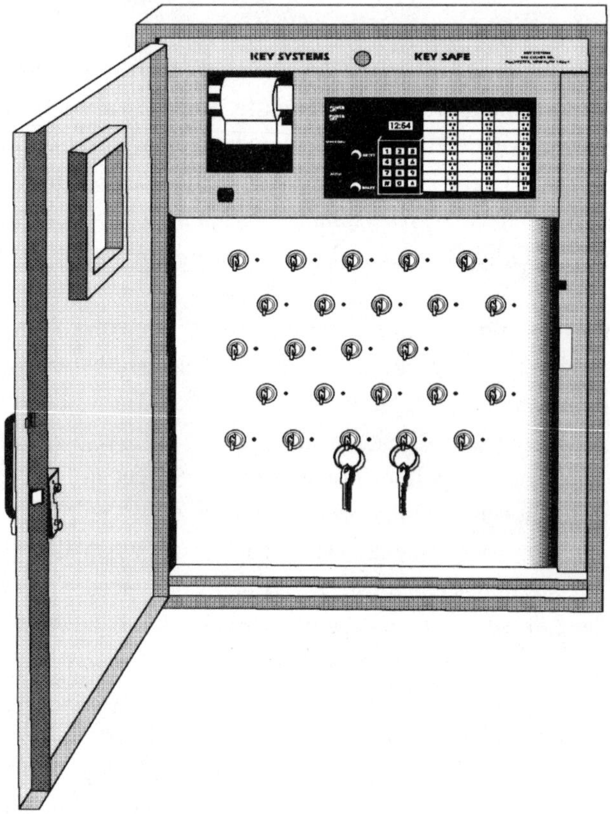

(*Source:* KEY Systems, Inc.)

FIGURE 2.23 Key Control Systems.

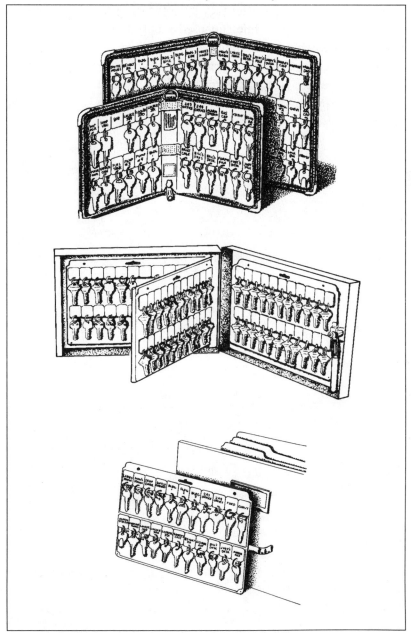

(*Source:* KEY Systems, Inc.)

opportunity to open rear doors and throw merchandise outside to an accomplice or for pickup after they leave the store. They won't be able to copy exit-door keys while supposedly only needing and using the key to a stockroom or other internal area.

If you are going to be away from the store for an extended period of time—on vacation, on a purchasing trip, or for medical reasons—leave your set of keys in the safe unless they are going to be used in your absence by a trustworthy manager.

PHYSICAL SECURITY CHECKLIST (PART ONE)

Doors, Windows, and Other Openings

☐ Protect all doors, windows, and other openings to the premises with locks, alarms, or both.

☐ Make sure all door frames are sturdy and in good condition.

☐ Make sure all doors are hung properly. They should fit in the frames snugly with the hinges well secured, and the hinge pins should be protected from easy removal.

☐ Install supplemental locking devices on all rear and side doors.

☐ Designate only one door as the primary point-of-entry.

☐ Make sure all windows that do not need to be opened occasionally are permanently closed and bolted to their frames. In addition, protect them by installing steel bars and wire screening.

☐ Secure with locks any windows that must be opened occasionally.

☐ Lock and install alarms on all ventilation shafts, air ducts, skylights, and trap doors.

☐ Examine the common walls adjoining other businesses, to ensure that no crawl spaces allow surreptitious entry into your store.

Locks and Keys

☐ Examine the locks on all doors, to ensure that they are of the proper type and that they are properly installed.

☐ Reinforce latch bolt locks by installing a more secure dead bolt lock.

(Continued)

(Continued)

☐ Use key-operated locks of the pin tumbler and interchangeable core cylinder type.

☐ Install all dead bolt locks with at least a 2-inch extension.

☐ Securely mount the strike plate into which the dead bolt fits with long (at least 2½- to 3-inch) screws.

☐ Make sure the locks to all perimeter doors—other than the one point-of-entry door—are inoperable from the outside.

☐ Use only padlocks made of hardened steel. If they are not of the combination type, make sure they operate with a pin tumbler mechanism.

☐ Ensure that mounting hasps for padlocks are sturdy, well secured, and of the type that, when in place, conceals the mounting screws.

☐ Pay special attention to locks installed on fire exits, to ensure they can be opened immediately in case of emergency.

☐ Properly lock offices, stockrooms, cash drawers, and cabinets containing security-sensitive or high-value merchandise.

☐ Equip your primary point-of-entry door with a time lock, to detect unauthorized entries after the store is closed.

☐ Establish a key plan by keying the locks for different degrees or levels of access.

☐ Maintain a log of keys. Require employees to sign receipts for all keys issued.

☐ Conduct periodic key inventories.

☐ Properly secure unissued and spare keys.

(Continued)

☐ Instruct all employees in proper key control procedures.

☐ Segregate store management keys and give managers only those keys necessary for the daily operation of the store.

☐ Consider replacing key-operated locks with combination, pushbutton, or magnetic card reader locking devices.

CHAPTER THREE

Alarm Systems and Other Physical Security Measures

E very business needs a variety of detection and alarm systems. Rarely does a retail establishment *not* require the installation of some type of burglar alarm, day alarm, holdup alarm, merchandise alarm, or fire and smoke alarm.

Alarm systems come in a wide variety of configurations ranging from the simple to the highly sophisticated and technically advanced. The location of your store, the type and value of your merchandise, and the depth of your pocketbook will be the significant factors in your decision as to what types of systems are best suited for you and your business. A list of alarm system companies is provided in the Appendix.

There are three basic types of alarms and signaling devices:

1. **Local alarms** sound a siren, bell, or loud horn on the premises or in the immediate vicinity of the area or merchandise being protected.

2. **Central station alarms** are silent at the premises but, instead, transmit a signal through leased telephone lines to the police or to a private central station monitoring office.

3. **Direct dial alarms** work through electronic devices and existing telephone lines to send prerecorded messages to protection agencies, police and fire departments, and others.

Let's examine the adaptability of these various systems and devices to the retail store environment and, at the same time, take a closer look at their basic structures and general use.

BURGLAR ALARMS

Burglar alarm systems are generally two-stage configurations consisting of a primary or perimeter alarm system and a secondary or space alarm system.

The Perimeter Alarm System

This is the most common and most familiar alarm system. It protects against unauthorized entry through the exterior shell of the premises. Protection is provided by the use of magnetic contact devices and magnetic foil tape affixed to all doors and windows that can be opened. Figure 3.1 shows the wide variety of applications suitable for such devices.

Sound, vibration, and motion detection alarm devices can also be used to monitor penetrations through roofs, walls, and large expanses of glass. Ventilation shafts, skylights, and trap doors leading to the roof can be alarmed in the same manner. These areas can also be protected by the use of alarmed wire traps.

A variation of the trap, a switch mat, is a thin, wired, matlike device that, when stepped on, sends an alarm. Because they are concealed under carpets in entryways, foyers, and hallways, and on stairways, switch mats are well worth considering as alternatives to the easily damaged magnetic foil tape alarm sensors.

FIGURE 3.1 Magnetic Contact Applications.

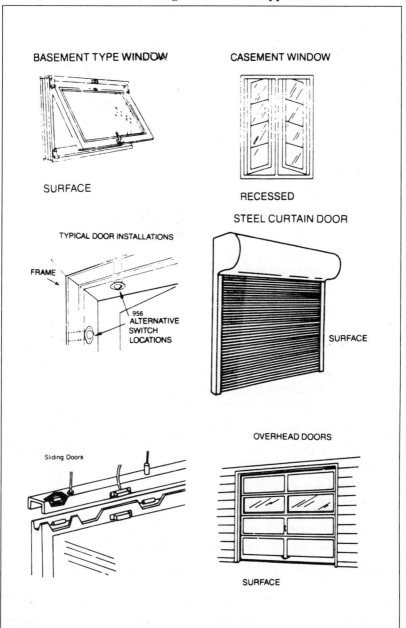

(*Source:* ADEMCO, Division of Pittway Corp.)

The Space Alarm System

Also known as an intrusion detection system, the space alarm system provides a secondary defensive zone. It is designed to detect intruders who have been able to penetrate the basic perimeter system. It will detect, for example, the movements of burglars who have gained entry by defeating the locking systems or by crawling through air shafts and through false ceilings from adjoining establishments. It will also detect "hide-ins" and "bust-outs"—thieves who hide and remain in the store after closing, gather up money and merchandise, and then break out to be picked up by accomplices.

Space alarms range from relatively simple mechanisms to technically sophisticated systems. Without going overboard with technical jargon, these alarms are described as follows:

- **Photoelectric systems.** Commonly used to open doors, these systems consist of a light beam aimed at a receiving cell, and the activation of an electrical current. When the light beam is broken, an alarm is transmitted.

- **Passive infrared motion detection systems.** These are similar to photoelectric systems except that the infrared beam of light is invisible. Changes in infrared energy, caused by an intruder's breaking the beam, will activate the alarm.

- **Ultrasonic motion detection systems.** Inaudible ultrasonic sound waves are transmitted into a specific zoned area. Any movement within the zone is reflected back to the sending unit, causing the alarm to be activated.

- **Microwave motion detection systems.** Similar to ultrasonic systems, these systems can be zoned to cover specific areas. They work on the same frequency shift or an interruption principle (the Doppler effect).

Ultrasonic and microwave motion detection systems have both advantages and disadvantages. On the plus side, they are excellent devices for detecting intruders inside the store, and they can be zoned; that is, an entire store can be protected, or coverage can be confined to critical areas such as offices, stockrooms, and high-value merchandise departments. On the minus side, they are frequently plagued by false alarms caused by a variety of stimuli: noise and vibrations from within or outside the store, power failures, birds, and air currents from heating and air-conditioning ducts. Most false alarms, however, are caused by user error, poor or inappropriate installation, and inferior equipment.

Regardless of their occasional problems, secondary intrusion detection systems contribute significantly to a total physical security protection package. Their installation, however, is not a "do-it-yourself" job; too many things have to be closely looked at and taken into consideration during the planning, device selection, and installation stages. The services of a professional alarm installation firm are highly recommended.

Choosing a Burglar Alarm System

Should your burglar alarm system use the local alarm or the central station alarm type of notification system? The answer depends on your goals and your operational environment. Do you just want to scare burglars away or do you want to catch them?

Local alarms, which ring loud bells that can be heard throughout the neighborhood, work well provided there are neighbors around at night to hear them, and provided that said neighbors, if they are not fed up with false alarms and the failures of store management to come and cut off the sleep-killing noise, will call the police and not assume, as too often happens, that someone else has already called.

Although local alarms are the least expensive of the notification systems, they should be used only in areas where response times can be rapid, such as in shopping centers with security patrols or in metropolitan areas with high degrees of municipal police coverage.

Silent, central station alarm systems are preferable. They are more expensive to install and maintain, but they usually pay for themselves in the long run. Activated without the knowledge of the intruder, they allow the police in quick-response areas to catch burglars in the act of breaking in or while they are inside the store, which makes arrest and prosecution easier. Silent alarms have a strong deterrent effect. The fact that a store has an effective alarm system spreads very quickly and greatly reduces the possibility that the same store will be targeted in the future.

Never let the installation of a burglar alarm system lull you into a false sense of security. Many professional thieves today are technology-literate and have been able to defeat or compromise most alarm systems. Frequent alarm examinations and tests are recommended, and a backup system may be advisable.

Warning! Be alert to individuals posing as alarm system salespersons or alarm maintenance personnel, who ask to inspect your system. They could very well be information gatherers for burglars. Check them out.

DAY ALARMS

Compared to the alarm systems previously mentioned, day alarms, or open-hours alarms, serve a completely different purpose. Day alarms are installed to detect break-outs, not break-ins. They are installed on exit doors to provide additional protection against shoplifting during periods when the store is open for business. Day alarms alert store management or security if someone attempts to steal merchandise and exit through one of the alarmed doors. There are two basic types of day alarms—the local alarm and the remote alarm.

The Local Alarm

As its name implies, the local alarm is constructed as part of the door-locking mechanism. A loud bell or buzzer sounds when someone pushes the panic bar or paddle locking the door. These devices come in a wide variety of configurations and designs. One of the more desirable features found on some of these exit device alarms is a delay feature. When the panic bar that opens the door is pushed, the alarm will sound but there will be about a 15-second delay before the door itself opens. The delay, while still providing for almost immediate exit in case of emergencies, will allow time for store management to quickly respond and check for unauthorized door openings. Examples of some local exit door alarms are depicted in Figure 3.2.

Remote Alarms

Remote alarms are usually installed on fire exits and other exterior doors. These exits are located so far away from the main selling floor that the local alarms built into the doors—for example, the locksets built into fire exit doors—cannot be heard. Remote alarm devices usually consist of a second set of magnetic contacts similar to those used in the primary burglar alarm system. The result, essentially, is a separate secondary alarm system; instead of being activated after closing, it is active while the store is open for business.

The control box, which turns the system on or off via a toggle switch or key, and which contains the sounding device, is the heart of this system and, unfortunately, may be its weak link. If the store owner or manager does not exercise vigilance over the control box to ensure that the system will only be turned off for controlled functions, such as deliveries and trash removal, the store will soon become the victim not only of shoplifters, but, unfortunately and frequently, of dishonest employees working independently or in concert with confederates.

HOLDUP ALARMS

Almost all holdup alarms are central station or direct dial alarms—they send silent signals or prerecorded messages to police or protection agencies, informing them that a holdup is in progress. The switches activating these alarms are usually installed in manager's offices, in cashier's cages, and at cash register locations. They may be pushbutton, knife-switch, foot-pad, or other pressure-sensitive devices.

Store owners can utilize another type of holdup alert: the "buddy system." If you are fortunate enough to be able to enlist the cooperation of another store owner, preferably one located next to you, it is relatively simple to set up a two-way buzzer system. Each merchant

FIGURE 3.2 Local Exit Door Alarms.

(*Source:* Alarm Lock Systems, Inc.)

buddy has in his store, or carries on his person, a panic transmitter with one or more buttons that can be pressed in case of a holdup or emergency. Depressing one buddy's button activates the alarm, and a low-key buzz sounds in the neighboring store, alerting the other store owner–buddy to investigate discreetly what might be going on and to call the police if such action appears warranted. The neighbor could also take down the license plate number and description of any car seen speeding away from the area.

SPECIFIC OBJECT AND MERCHANDISE ALARMS

A safe is a specific object that should be protected by an alarm. Space alarms that detect sound or motion can provide adequate protection in most instances, but a business owner wishing to protect safes containing large amounts of money or exceptionally valuable merchandise, such as fine jewelry, should consider other options. In addition to safes that can only be opened at specific times, there are now on the market electronic proximity and vibration detection alarms that send signals to the police or to a central station if the slightest motion or vibration to the object is sensed.

Another type of alarm is activated by the presence of human body heat. These newer types of alarms are often used to protect valuable pieces of art and high-value technical and scientific equipment.

The average store owner does not usually need such technically advanced and expensive alarm systems. Merchandise on sales floors can usually be protected by the use of showcase locks, security cables, and, as necessary, a wide variety of electronic antishoplifting disks, tags, and devices.

Safes

Before moving on to the next category of alarms, let's expand a bit on the subject of safes. As the repositories for the lifeblood of the business—the money—safes deserve some additional attention. Not only should they be alarmed and fire-resistant, but some thought should go into their placement, installation, usage, and access.

Unless you have a vault-type safe that is built into the structure of the building itself, have the safe bolted to the floor when it is installed. This anchoring is especially important if the safe is located up front, near a window. Countless numbers of safes have been removed by burglars who, using a tow truck, back up through a window, hook up the safe, and jerk it away. It is then broken into at their leisure, at some remote location. The contents are stolen and the smashed shell of the safe is thrown away.

Open the safe only when necessary. When it is not in use, lock it. Don't just close the door; spin the dial on the combination lock (which, of course, every safe should have). Protect the combination carefully. Don't write it down on a desk pad or a calendar, or in an address book, even if you attempt to disguise it as a telephone number. Memorize it! And give it out very judiciously. **The more people who have access to the safe, the more difficult it will be to establish responsibility in case of loss.**

Give some consideration to how you use your safe and the nature of its contents. If, in addition to cash, money orders, and similar negotiables, the bulk of the material you retain in the safe consists of the company books, documentation, and computer disks (keep backup copies off-premises), you should look into the possibility of using a dual-compartment safe. You would have a high-security compartment protected by a combination lock for the money and valuables, and a separate, larger compartment, protected by another lock, for the documentation and other bulkier items. Compartmentalized safes offer an additional method to restrict access to the contents.

FIRE, SMOKE, AND EQUIPMENT ALARMS

The types of basic fire alarms you install in your store are going to be dictated by the local fire marshal in fulfillment of local laws and ordinances. Enhanced systems, as long as they do not violate any local ordinance, may be installed at your discretion, depending on your operational environment and the types of merchandise you carry.

Tremendous advances have been made in fire and smoke detection systems. Some are now so sensitive that they can literally "sense" fire, "hear" flames, and detect the slightest wisp or whiff of smoke.

Generally, these detection devices work on the photoelectricity or ionization principle. Some have interchangeable sensing units and can work either way. The alarms are calibrated to sense a buildup of heat, the presence of smoke, and the fumes and by-products of a fire, whether of the fast burning or smoldering type.

Rate-of-rise and fixed-temperature thermostats are also available. These secondary devices are commonly used in boiler rooms, trash rooms, and areas where overheating machinery or spontaneous combustion is a hazard.

As with burglar alarms, fire and smoke alarms can be installed to sound an alert on the premises and to immediately send a signal to a central station monitoring unit. To provide for the safety of customers and employees, all large stores should also install fire alarm pull stations, especially in rear storage areas.

In addition to fire and smoke alarms, many stores require alarm systems to monitor various functions and equipment. It doesn't take long, for example, for a grocer to suffer a large loss if the refrigeration system fails. Other equipment frequently monitored includes boilers, generators, elevators, sump pumps, and fuel supplies. The potential for water leaks or the possible presence of toxic gases is reason enough to install this kind of alarm protection.

CLOSED-CIRCUIT TELEVISION SYSTEMS

Closed-circuit television (CCTV) is essentially a monitoring system, but it can, and frequently does, serve also as a visual alarm. In addition to video taping armed robberies, CCTV is very useful in monitoring rear entrances, shipping and receiving docks, and sales floor. It can also be a great aid in detecting dishonesty among employees, especially cashiers. The biggest drawback to CCTV systems is that they are relatively expensive and require additional personnel for the actual monitoring. When properly installed and staffed, however, they can serve as very worthwhile deterrent devices.

LIGHTING

Adequate lighting, of both the interior and the exterior is a strong deterrent to break-ins. Sufficient interior lights should be left on at night so that police patrols and other passersby can see what is going on inside your store. Don't negate this advantage by putting so many merchandise and sale signs on the windows that looking into the store becomes impossible. *Make sure you have a battery-operated backup lighting system that immediately activates when interruptions to your normal power system occur.* A secondary gasoline- or diesel-fuel-operated generator is even better.

The exterior—the front and rear, plus any side entrances—should be well lighted. Burglars do not like to be in a spotlight. Locate the lights high enough so that the bulbs cannot be easily removed or broken. Lighting fixtures are available with wire mesh grills and shatterproof glass, which make them impervious to breakage from stones and pellet guns.

FIRE, ELECTRICAL, AND WATER HAZARDS

Nothing is quite so dispiriting as the first morning-after look at a store that has been reduced to smoldering rubble by an overnight fire. It is especially gut-wrenching if there is any realization that the fire could have been prevented.

Don't wait until your local fire marshal comes around to make an annual inspection—check things out yourself. Make a formal tour on at least a quarterly basis, and observe the following daily fire prevention precautions:

- **If smoking in retail stores is not already illegal in your area, discourage smoking in your store.** Prohibit it entirely if you can. Do not allow smoking in the storerooms, rest rooms, or trash rooms. If allowed in coffee-break areas or lunchrooms, insist that employees use glass or ceramic ashtrays and not paper or styrofoam cups. At closing time, check the contents of all ashtrays and trash cans, and look beneath all tables and chairs for any smoldering butts.

- **Make sure that merchandise is not stacked against or too near incandescent light bulbs.** At least 24 inches of space is recommended. The same holds true of placing merchandise, particularly janitorial supplies, paints, and other chemicals, near hot water heaters, motors, and electrical devices or outlets.

- **Check for signs of frayed wiring on cash registers, lighting fixtures, and electrically operated displays.** Instruct your employees to be alert for such hazards. Check the main electric panels in the store. If they are hot or seem unusually warm, notify your electrician immediately.

- **If you must use portable heaters to keep your sales personnel warm in exposed locations, exercise extreme caution.** Be sure to give the heaters adequate clearance. Keep them away from trash cans, paper bags, and other inflammables. At closing time, be positive that the heater is not just turned off, but that the plug on the line cord is pulled from the outlet box. If an extension cord must be used, be sure it is of the proper type and that it and the entire circuit into which it is plugged during work hours can carry the increased electrical load.

- **Keep clear all rear areas and hallways leading to fire exits.** Fire exit doors must be able to be opened from the inside by means of a panic bar. They must not be locked during business hours. In fact, in many jurisdictions, not even secondary locks to protect against break-ins during nonoperating hours are allowed to be locked during business hours. Check with your local fire marshal for the restrictions that are in effect in your area. These restrictions are another reason why fire exit doors should be tied into both your primary alarm system and your day alarm system.

- **Locate fire extinguishers in every store, in conformance with local fire regulations.** Extinguishers should be available for ready access near front and rear exits, stockrooms, basement areas, and heating and electrical equipment. Although most of them require recharging only on an annual basis, check them periodically throughout the year. Know how to operate them. Be sure that all employees know the location of the fire extinguisher nearest to their duty stations, and, equally important, that they know how to use it. Test them.

- **Install fire and smoke detectors.** Test them periodically.
- **Develop evacuation procedures and train all employees.**
- **If it ever should become necessary to evacuate the store because of a fire, attempt to do it in a calm, orderly manner.** Customers exit first, through rear fire exit doors if necessary. Two preappointed searchers, one male and one female, should check the rest rooms, stockrooms, and other areas, to alert customers and employees who may not be aware of the danger. Lock the office funds in your fireproof safe. Collect and lock up the cash register receipts, if time permits. If not, tell your employees to lock their registers and to give you the keys. As employees evacuate the store, designate a meeting place where they are to remain until you can check later and be sure they are all accounted for.
- **Immediately after a fire, rope off the affected area, or erect barriers to prevent unauthorized persons from entering.** This cordoning off is necessary not only to prevent injury but also to protect against theft and vandalism. Be especially watchful that cleanup crews do not "accidentally" remove undamaged or salvageable merchandise along with the rubble. Regretfully, it is also recommended that you keep your eye on the firefighters. Most are completely trustworthy, but there have been incidents where merchandise was pocketed, secreted in boots, or removed from the store while gathering up firefighting equipment and hoses after a fire.

Preventing Water Damage

The concluding topic in this chapter on hazards is the potential losses caused by water. It is amazing how much damage to merchandise, fixtures, ceilings, and carpeting can be done in one night by an over-flowing sink. Make sure at closing time that all faucets are turned off. Check the rest rooms to see that commodes are not overflowing or that some disgruntled employee or vandal has not plugged up the basins and left the water running. If any old, rust-encrusted water or sewage pipes are observed, determine whether they are beginning to leak, a sign that they may be about to burst. In cold climates, adequately protect exposed pipes from freezing.

PHYSICAL SECURITY CHECKLIST (PART TWO)

Alarms

☐ Install burglar alarms to protect against unauthorized entry through the exterior shell of the premises.

☐ Install space alarm systems to detect intruders who have been able to penetrate the basic perimeter system.

☐ Install a silent, central station type of alarm system.

☐ Install a day alarm, or open-hours alarm, system to detect break-outs and unauthorized exits by employees.

☐ Install holdup alarms.

☐ Make sure the safe is protected by a proximity or vibration detection alarm.

☐ Install fire and smoke alarms.

Lighting

☐ Check that the exterior of the store is adequately lighted at night, especially the areas surrounding all doors and windows.

☐ Make sure the interior of the store is sufficiently lighted at night, so that police patrols and other passersby can see what is going on inside the store.

☐ Install an emergency lighting system.

Fire, Electrical, and Water Hazards

☐ Educate all employees on all fire, electrical, and water hazards.

☐ As applicable, follow all safety recommendations provided in this chapter.

PART TWO

External Loss Prevention

This part describes how to prevent losses caused by external forces, that is, by nonemployees. Chief among these forces are shoplifters, armed robbers, bad-check passers, and fraudulent credit card users. In a secondary category are fast-change and con artists, counterfeiters, dishonest vendors, and criminals who engage in a wide variety of exchange and refund schemes.

Burglars are certainly an external force, but defensive actions to thwart their efforts were covered in Chapter 2. With the exception of armed robberies that occur away from the store or are the result of "hide-ins" and after-hours calls to come back to the store, the chapters in this Part center on the external forces that operate against you while your store is open for business.

In addressing losses of this type, you must be knowledgeable about the techniques utilized and the governing laws and legal issues involved. You need this knowledge for your own use and protection and as a means of informing and training your employees. Without question, an alert and trained work force can be your best external loss prevention asset.

CHAPTER FOUR

Shoplifting

S tatistics compiled by the FBI indicate that shoplifting is one of the fastest-growing larcenies in this country. Annual losses to businesses from this crime are estimated to be in the billions of dollars. Given the wide-open, self-service environment existing in most retail establishments, these figures should not come as any surprise. Shoplifting is likely to continue to affect your profits—unless you do something about it. Your losses from shoplifting can be reduced. All it takes is a better understanding of the problem, a knowledge of the legal issues involved, and implementation of some proven preventive measures. The information in this chapter should help.

TYPES OF SHOPLIFTERS

Shoplifters, or "boosters" as they are commonly known, come in all sizes and shapes, represent every age group, and come from all socioeconomic levels. Professionals do it for a living; narcotic addicts do it to support their habits; kleptomaniacs do it to satisfy a compulsive urge; and neurotics do it for revenge or to "get even" for some imagined slight. Sadly, the elderly, the unemployed, and the housewife shoplift to supplement family budgets. Juveniles do it to stretch their allowances, as initiation into clubs, or just for "kicks." In short, everyone who comes into your store could be a potential shoplifter.

METHODS UTILIZED

The methods and techniques utilized by shoplifters to separate you from your merchandise are limited only by their imagination and resourcefulness, which, unfortunately, they have in great abundance. The specific acts may vary, depending on the circumstances, but shoplifting is usually carried out in one of three ways: (1) sleight-of-hand, (2) devices, and (3) distraction.

Sleight-of-Hand

This method, also known as "palming" is the most common method used, especially by nonprofessionals. Items are simply and quickly taken by hand and concealed in sleeves, pockets, or purses, or dropped into shopping bags or other packages.

Devices

For the most part, devices are used almost exclusively by professional shoplifters. A schoolgirl who secretes a tube of lipstick in a hollowed out schoolbook is technically using a device, but the ones we are focusing on here are much more elaborate and devious. For example, a wide variety of "booster coats" feature a number of pockets and hooks sewn into the lining, enabling them to hold and conceal great quantities of merchandise. A companion garment is the "booster bloomer," a large undergarment tied at the bottom around each leg and worn under loose fitting clothing. An amazing number of silk dresses can be dropped into and concealed in such a device. There are also "booster boxes." Such devices are disguised to look like ordinary garment boxes, boxes ready for mailing, or gift boxes. Their unique feature is that the bottom or one end is false or spring-operated. The shoplifter places the box on or near the targeted item, pushes it against the box, and, like magic, it disappears.

Some shoplifters are known as "crotch carriers." They can carry out merchandise between their upper legs. A proficient professional can carry out astonishingly heavy and bulky items in this manner. Many professionals use slings under their clothing, to support extra heavy loads.

Strollers and baby carriages, especially the older, larger types, are the favorite devices of many female professional shoplifters. The carriages are modified so that the mattress or pad on which the baby rests is raised, leaving a large space underneath for the concealment of shoplifted merchandise. In many cases, the "baby" in the carriage is a doll, not a real baby.

Distraction

This is a favorite method used by shoplifting professionals. Working in pairs or in larger groups, these individuals employ a wide variety to ruses to distract managers and sales personnel from their duties. Some ruses are very simple. For example, a pair will come into a department area and, while one engages the salesperson in showing merchandise or in retrieving an item from a stockroom, the other team member does the shoplifting. Groups that create disturbances by engaging in loud arguments and mock fights among themselves, or having a member of the group fake a fainting spell or a seizure, are much more imaginative. While everyone clusters around to see what is going on, the rest of the team is cleaning out the store.

Another type of shoplifter—the so-called "clean" shoplifter— does not fit into any of the above categories. Clean shoplifters are not really shoplifters at all; they just want you to think they are. Most of them act suspiciously, and then openly take and conceal merchandise. They subsequently leave the items elsewhere in the store, or pass them off to an accomplice, before being confronted by some unwary manager or salesperson. When stopped and confronted, and found to be "clean," they initiate civil lawsuits for false arrest, malicious prosecution, or defamation of character. Settlements for large amounts of money are usually the outcome of such tactics.

SUSPICIOUS SIGNALS

If you know what to watch for, a very large percentage of potential shoplifting acts can be prevented. Figure 4.1 lists some guidelines of what to watch for. Consider posting these guidelines in the back of your store as a reminder to employees.

PREVENTIVE MEASURES

The operative word here is *preventive*. Except in those rare cases when you really want to catch someone in the act and make an arrest, your goal should be preventing shoplifting, not watching it occur. To successfully accomplish this goal, however, you must have a dedicated

FIGURE 4.1   How to Spot Shoplifters—Customers to Watch Out For.

- Customers who spend more time in watching to see where you and your salespeople are than they do in looking at the merchandise. Remember, before thieves can steal, they have to check to see whether they are being observed.
- Customers who loiter, handle a lot of merchandise, but make no apparent attempt to purchase.
- Shoppers who wear oversized and baggy clothing or who wear or carry overcoats or raincoats when the weather does not call for them.

(Continued)

FIGURE 4.1   *(Continued)*

- Customers who seem nervous or ill at ease and do not want any assistance.

- Customers who linger around counters located near exits. Many professional shoplifters "work the exits," where they can grab merchandise and get out quickly, usually to speed off in an automobile driven by an accomplice.

- People who carry large, empty, or nearly empty shopping bags or purses, especially those who walk around with their purses open. Watch, also, those who carry umbrellas. When in the upside-down, partially open position, they become natural hiding places.

- Customers who keep sending you away from the counter or from the department area to a back stockroom to check for other sizes, colors, or styles. Alert another salesperson or rapidly double-back on them.

- Shoppers who walk around the store with large, unwrapped items such as luggage or boxed merchandise into which other items may be concealed.

- Customers who attempt to get behind sales counters or into back hallways or stockroom areas.

- Customers with baby carriages and strollers.

- Youngsters who come into the store in groups; juvenile shoplifting as the result of a dare or peer pressure is most likely among groups.

- Persons who create disturbances in the store. They may be part of a professional team. While everyone is attracted to the disturbance, other members of the team are busy shoplifting. Look around; see what is going on elsewhere.

- Very early and very late or last-minute shoppers. Many professional shoplifters strike when sales personnel are preoccupied with their checking-in and checking-out duties.

and knowledgable management staff and a motivated, trained, and alert sales force. A variety of shoplifting deterrent devices and the creation and use of certain psychological procedures and barriers will also assist you in developing and broadcasting a reputation as a "tight" store, one that will be avoided by shoplifters. Some guidelines are provided in the following sections.

Customer Relations

Train all employees to carry out the following procedures:

- **Promptly acknowledge the presence of all persons who enter the store or department area.** Even if you are engaged with another customer, make some comment, such as "Good morning, Ma'am," or "I'll be with you in a moment, Sir." Your true customers will appreciate your interest. Others, intent on shoplifting, will know that they have been observed and that you are watching them.

- **Give quick service.** It greatly reduces the opportunity and the temptation to steal and is especially important where juveniles are concerned.

- **Assist customers who carry merchandise around the store in their hands.** Offer to help them by holding the items or by getting a shopping cart. If you happen to see an item being dropped into a pocket or a purse, mention it by name. For example, "May I hold these items and that lipstick for you?"

- **Instruct and periodically remind all cashiers to check the lower racks of shopping carts.** Look inside such items as trash cans, picnic chests, and tool boxes for merchandise customers may have "forgotten" to place on the checkout counter.

- **Instruct all sales personnel to pause right at the subtotal point, when ringing up a sale for a customer.** While looking the customer in the eye, they should ask, "Is there anything else?," and pause until the customer responds. This is one of the most effective psychological deterrents to shoplifting and one of the easiest to implement. The number of items pulled from pockets and purses will be amazing.

- **Instruct all sales personnel not to leave their department areas unattended.** An unattended or understaffed department is an open invitation to steal.

Merchandise Handling

The following tips can also prevent shoplifting:

- **Protect high-value merchandise.** When possible, keep such merchandise in locked storerooms and display only samples. If your line of merchandise precludes taking such precautions, use locked showcases or retain high-value items behind staffed service counters. Do not display high-value merchandise near exits. Also, despite their uninviting appearance and the fact that they offend many true customers, chained and alarmed devices may have to be installed to protect some electronic equipment, appliances, expensive designer fashions, and fur coats.

- **Display merchandise neatly.** Organized displays make it easier to spot missing items. The same holds true for arranging and presenting counter-top merchandise for customer examination and selection. Customers should be shown only one valuable item at a time. Beware of "switching," especially if you are in the jewelry trade. Professionals frequently attempt to switch your valuable diamonds or gemstones with their similarly mounted, cut-glass imitations. If at all possible, do not turn your back on customers when getting merchandise for them.

- **Know the prices of your merchandise.** "Ticket switching" is a commonly used technique. Sales personnel should be instructed to double-check prices before ringing up any unusual "bargains." When possible, double-price all big-ticket items, especially those with easily switched string tags. Place the second recording of the price in an inconspicuous location, and inform all sales personnel to check these secondary pricing locations before recording the sale.

- **To deter ticket switching, use firmly attached plastic string tags, or price stickers that peel off in pieces if tampered with.** If tickets must be stapled on, use a distinctive stapling pattern that is recognizable to store personnel. When restocking merchandise, do not leave price stickers or tags lying about. You risk having some taken by dishonest individuals and placed on much more expensive merchandise.

- **When possible, mark merchandise so that it can be identified as store property.** Besides being vital in handling an apprehended shoplifter, such information can greatly increase the amount of merchandise recovered, even in undiscovered thefts. Much stolen property recovered by police cannot be returned because it cannot be traced to the store from which it was stolen. Stamp items with a company logo or a coded serial number. Some high-value merchandise can also be marked with ultraviolet crayon or ink.

- **Don't use a pen or pencil to note the new price of sale or markdown merchandise on original sales tags.** You are openly inviting thieves to do likewise. Make new tickets or take the markdowns at the cash register.

- **Control fitting rooms—an absolute must if you are in the retail clothing trade.** If unattended, fitting rooms should be locked. An accurate count of the merchandise each customer takes into a fitting room should be made. The garments themselves should be closely observed, to preclude the switching and concealing of, for example, an expensive dress for another that is much less costly.

Store Layouts

The manner in which a store is laid out and the merchandise is displayed plays a large role in deterring shoplifters. Consider the following design ideas to deter shoplifters:

- **Keep your displays low enough so that the location of all customers can readily be seen.** High fixtures and tall displays create protective screening and induce shoplifting.

- **Plan and coordinate the placement of your cash registers and customer service counters with your fixtures and displays so as to maximize sales floor coverage.** Create as many "line of sight" settings as possible, and strive for "overlaps" where two or more employees can observe displays of high-value merchandise.

- **Try to arrange the store so that everyone leaving must pass a checkout counter.**

- **Close and block off unused checkout aisles.**

- **Limit the number of exits.**

- **Depending on the nature and floor plan of your store, locate the manager's office where it will deter shoplifters (and dishonest employees).** If possible, construct an elevated office, partially enclosed with opaque one-way glass, at the front of the store near the checkout register closest to the exit. From such a vantage point, you should be able to see the entire sales floor. Even when the office is unoccupied, the use of one-way glass will deter potential shoplifters because they won't know whether they are being observed.

Deterrent Devices and Systems

Consider installing any or all of the following types of deterrent devices:

- **Electronic sensing devices.** Great technological strides have been made in the development of a wide variety of electronic sensing devices to deter shoplifting. These tags and embedded sensors are among the most effective of the deterrent systems, but they are expensive and time-consuming to install and remove. In addition, they require close monitoring of the exit stations by trained sales or security personnel. Failure to remove or deactivate the sensors during the course of legitimate sales can annoy and embarrass honest customers and lead to false arrest or defamation of character suits. In spite of these drawbacks, if your line of merchandise includes high-value clothing items, you must consider the use of sensors as a part of your primary deterrent program.

- **Convex mirrors.** Strategically placed convex mirrors can be an asset in making observations around tall displays and into hard-to-see corners. Their advantages, however, are marginal. They allow shoplifters to watch for employees, and they cause visual distortions, making it very difficult to accurately observe what a potential shoplifter may be doing or concealing.

- **Flat mirrors.** The generous use of regular, flat mirrors mounted on pillars and walls is recommended. A long expanse of flat mirror mounted at the juncture of the rear wall and ceiling, and canted slightly downward, will, in most small to medium-size stores, provide excellent coverage of the entire sales floor. Not only will such mirrors inhibit shoplifting, they will also help supervisors in monitoring the actions of other store personnel.

- **Observation posts.** These utilize one-way mirrors and peepholes in offices and back rooms and in columns. They can be very effective in detecting shoplifters. Unfortunately, they also have disadvantages. They are expensive to maintain because they must be staffed by someone at the observation post and by a colleague on the sales floor.

- **Closed circuit television (CCTV) systems.** CCTV systems have the same cost drawback as observation posts. Although very effective, maintaining and utilizing CCTV systems properly may be prohibitive. Some store owners have resorted to the installation of "dummy" cameras, but this subterfuge has had only marginal success. Once shoplifters realize the system is bogus, their efforts increase tenfold.

If you intend to install a real, working CCTV system, be prepared to spend a considerable amount of money for installation, maintenance, and personnel to operate the system properly. Think carefully about where to place the monitoring portion of the system. Most such monitoring stations are located off the sales floor—in offices and back rooms.

If shoplifting is a major problem and you want to make a significant deterrent impact, there is a remedy—if you can live with it. Construct a glass-walled monitoring station just inside your main entrance. Hook up a dozen or so TVs inside the station, and have them monitored by a uniformed security officer. Make sure that both the monitors and the security officer are positioned so that they can be seen by everyone who enters the store. Such an installation makes a tremendous visual impact. However, it also totally destroys any semblance of the dignified professional ambiance you may be striving to maintain within the store, and wreaks havoc with your customer relations. In short, you have created a war zone.

- **Uniformed guards.** The use of uniformed guards is debatable. Their presence may deter some shoplifting by juveniles and amateurs, but they will have little or no effect on the professionals. In fact, the guards' presence may lead to an increase in shoplifting. Sales personnel may be deluded into a false sense of security and become less observant of activities on the sales floor—leading, in turn, to increased shoplifting. Uniformed guards are most effective when posted at exits. The best strategy, however, is to have the guards work in conjunction with plainclothes guards and detectives.

By far, the best shoplifting deterrent system is an alert, well-trained staff. To maximize their efforts, each store should develop an "alerting code" utilizing the store paging system or a similar communication method to summon supervisory or other floor personnel into a specific area when suspicious activity is observed. Such coding need not be elaborate but it should quickly and simply identify the department area in which additional coverage is needed. For example, a simple alerting system can be developed under the guise of an announcement of a telephone call for a store employee.

First, however, the sales floor area must be sectioned off, and each segment or clearly defined department area must be given an identity number that will serve as its coded location marker. Start at the front left and work your way across and down the length of store, ending in the right rear section. This numbered location grid then becomes the "telephone extension number" portion of your coded announcement. See Figure 4.2 for an example of such a coded store layout.

If your store already has clearly defined department areas and each one has its own telephone extension number, you can use the department's extension number as an area identifier instead of laying out a grid.

Once the store has been sectioned off and coded, this is how the system will work. When a salesperson or the store manager (in the elevated office) notices suspicious activity in a particular department area, an announcement is made: "Mr. Seward, you have a telephone call on extension 105." In this case, the fictional "Mr. Seward" is the code word for a security problem and "105" designates the exact location where assistance is needed. The first digit signifies the first floor and "05" gives the specific location as noted on the store identity grid, or the telephone extension number of a specific and identifiable department area. Upon hearing the announcement, floor supervisors and other personnel move into the area to provide additional coverage.

CONFRONTING, DETAINING, AND ARRESTING SHOPLIFTERS

Now for the hard part. What do you do if you or one of your staff actually see someone shoplift? The answer to that question brings into play a host of concerns, cautions, and legal caveats, all leading to one significant point: *Exercise extreme caution.* If you don't, you are surely going to pay for it.

For openers, bear in mind that not everyone who removes merchandise from your store without paying for it is a thief. The world is full of people who are senile, distraught, under the influence of adverse reactions from prescription drugs, mentally incompetent, preoccupied, or just plain absentminded. And many of them shop in your store. Do your best to evaluate the status and mental condition of anyone you confront

FIGURE 4.2   Antishoplifting Grid.

ACCESSORIES **Ext. 1**	**SPORTSWEAR** **Ext. 2**
DRESSES **Ext. 3**	**SUITS & COATS** **Ext. 4**
LINGERIE **Ext. 5**	**SHOES** **Ext. 6**

as a suspected shoplifter, and do not make an arrest or proceed with prosecutive action if it does not appear warranted. The adverse publicity your store could suffer, to say nothing of possible civil judgments against you if you lose your case, far outweighs any marginal benefits you might obtain.

On the other hand, there are certainly "customers" who do shoplift and who do intend to permanently deprive you of your goods. They are criminals, and you should strive to put them out of action. Prosecute every one you catch, even first-time offenders. They will all tell you that this is their first time. Don't believe them. A strong and firm prosecution policy goes a long way toward establishing that your store is "tough" on shoplifters. That in itself could very well become your most effective deterrent.

The road that begins at the observing of an act of shoplifting and ends with a prosecution is not a smooth one; it is cratered with potholes, detours, breakdowns, and legal radar traps. As a store manager, it is imperative that you learn to navigate this road.

Laws Relating to Shoplifting

Laws relating to shoplifting (technically, a larceny) vary from state to state and among local jurisdictions, but they all contain a certain degree of commonality. In order to prove that a crime has been committed, two elements must be present:

1. An act must have taken place that is prohibited by law (for example, the concealment of merchandise);

2. There must be provable intent—in a case of shoplifting, you must be able to show, beyond any reasonable doubt, that the person detained did not intend to pay for the merchandise concealed.

Before confronting any suspected shoplifters, determine the laws and proper procedural guidelines that exist in your operational area. Consult with your attorney and your servicing police departments, and obtain guidance and advice from the office of your District Attorney (or Commonwealth or local Prosecuting Attorney). Many of these agencies have preprinted shoplifting guidelines on hand, and some have community or business liaison officers who can introduce programs to assist you in training your staff.

Confronting and Detaining Shoplifters

Before you confront or detain someone you suspect of shoplifting, the following requirements absolutely, positively must be met:

- You, or the employee accompanying you in making the detention, must have seen the act of shoplifting take place.

- You, or that same employee, must have had the shoplifter *and the place of concealment* continuously in sight since the act occurred, and must be *absolutely certain* that the merchandise is still in the possession of the shoplifter.

- You must be certain that the merchandise involved is actually your store property.

- The individual must have demonstrated, by some overt act, that he or she has no intention to pay for the merchandise. The tearing off of a price tag or the concealment of an item while still on the sales floor constitutes an act of shoplifting in most jurisdictions, but much stronger proof of *intent to permanently deprive* can be obtained by allowing the shoplifter to exit the store before making the apprehension.

If you are not positive about all these issues—if there is the slightest doubt in your mind—do not make the stop. Do not, under any circumstances, make the stop if the individual, or even that portion of the individual where the merchandise was being concealed (a purse, a box, a stroller), has been out of your (or your employee's) constant line-of-sight, even if only for seconds. You are far better off losing the merchandise than being faced with a civil suit if you make the detention and then, belatedly, discover that your suspected shoplifter is "clean."

Shoplifters frequently realize or sense that they have been observed, and they get rid of the merchandise before being confronted. Some, as pointed out earlier, surreptitiously pass the merchandise off to accomplices. By the time they are stopped, they no longer have the items, and then, depending on your comments and actions at the time of the confrontation, they initiate legal action against you for false arrest. Bear in mind that the term false arrest does not pertain solely to actions by police officers. Once you stop and detain someone—that is, prevent the person from engaging in normal activities—you have, technically, made a "citizen's arrest." Before you act, be sure and be careful.

This entire issue of confronting and detaining suspected shoplifters is, unfortunately, often misunderstood. Unless you can fully explain it, you could easily wind up with a very disgruntled and disaffected sales staff. You must be able to tell them why you—and they—can take no action if, after they observe an act of shoplifting, they do not closely follow the shoplifter but, instead, go off looking for you, to report the theft. Proper training regarding this subject, for both supervisory and general sales personnel, cannot be overemphasized.

Arresting Shoplifters

If you are certain that all of the previously mentioned requirements have been met, you may then proceed with the actual detention and, if warranted, subsequent arrest. As a general rule, train all employees to follow the guidelines in Figure 4.3. Consider posting these guidelines in the back of the store, as a reminder to employees.

FIGURE 4.3   Guidelines for How to Arrest Shoplifters.

- **Be careful!!! Not all shoplifters react quietly to being arrested.** Many of them, especially the professionals and drug addicts, become violent and may carry firearms or other dangerous weapons. Many work with accomplices who will come to their aid if detained. **If you do not feel you can physically**
  (Continued)

FIGURE 4.3 *(Continued)*

handle the situation, do not attempt the arrest. Instead, obtain descriptions, vehicle identification data, and direction of travel, and immediately notify your local police department. If you do decide to physically restrain someone, bear in mind that if the suspect resists, you can use only the minimum amount of force necessary to overcome that resistance. When possible, have someone call the police before the actual apprehension takes place. Officers may be able to respond in time to provide assistance.

- **Attempt to have a witness to the shoplifting and, especially, to the detention.** Not only will this second person be able to help in safeguarding your personal safety, he or she will be in a position to hear any admissions made by the suspect.

- **Do not accuse the shoplifter of stealing or indicate that a "mistake" may have been made.** You may find you are wrong on both counts. Approach in a confident manner, identify yourself, and firmly state, "I believe you have some merchandise which you have forgotten to pay for. Would you return to the store with me, please?" Without waiting for a response, escort the suspect back into the store. Recover the merchandise before returning to the store, when possible. Note and remember where it was concealed.

- **Once you are back in the store, take the suspect to an office or private area.** If someone has not already done so, call the police. If you are fortunate, they will be able to respond and take over. They will conduct whatever interviews and interrogations are necessary, take written statements, and take custody of the evidence.

If, unfortunately, the police, for any number of very valid reasons, cannot respond in a reasonable amount of time or as a matter of department policy do not investigate shoplifting incidents, you will have to make a decision as to whether to interview the suspect yourself.

Interviewing Shoplifting Suspects

For the most part, interviewing suspected shoplifters is not all that difficult. They either have your merchandise or they don't. If you did not recover your merchandise at the time you made the detention or are not positive that they currently have it in their possession, you should not have made the stop or be interviewing them. If, on the other hand, you recovered the merchandise or are positive that they still have it and that you can obtain it by request or by conducting a lawful search, you have direct, prima facie evidence of the crime. Actually, in such cases, a lengthy interview and written admission of guilt, while desirable, is not absolutely necessary. As long as you have the evidence, the witnesses, and the identity of the shoplifter, you can obtain an arrest warrant. Getting the evidence and the true identity of the shoplifter, however, usually requires an interview.

There are many other good reasons for conducting interviews of shoplifting suspects. Among them are the following:

- To obtain an admission of guilt.
- To obtain a written, signed confession.
- To determine whether the suspect has other store merchandise on his or her person or in a vehicle, residence, or other location.
- To determine the identity of any accomplices.
- To learn the shoplifting techniques utilized, so that existing antishoplifting procedures can be reviewed and enhanced if necessary.
- To have the suspect sign a form releasing you and others from civil liability resulting from the detention and interrogation. (More on this subject later.)

Now that you have a better understanding of why you should conduct the interview, let's go over some basic procedural guidelines as to how it should be accomplished. Figure 4.4 provides a checklist. Again, consider posting these guidelines in the back of the store, to remind employees of proper interviewing procedures.

FIGURE 4.4   Guidelines for Interviewing Suspected Shoplifters.

- Identify yourself to the suspect.
- Take the suspect to an office or similar private area.
- Have another person present. If the suspected shoplifter is a female, your witness should also be a female.
- Recover the merchandise if it was not obtained during the detention. Make sure that the suspect does not discard it while being returned to the store. State the item(s) stolen and its place of concealment. This will usually convince the shoplifter that he or she has been caught red-handed. If it does not, courts have held that if you have reasonable cause to believe the suspect has your merchandise, you may legally conduct a search to recover it.
- Instruct the shoplifter to place on the desk or table all items not paid for. There may be other merchandise that you are not aware of.
- Do not make any threats and do not make any promises.
- Once you have decided to go ahead with the arrest, do not accept any payment for the merchandise.
- Obtain the full identification of the shoplifter, cross-checking it with documentation in his or her possession. Attempt to obtain identification cards with photographs and physical descriptions and compare them with your suspect. Many professional shoplifters carry false or stolen identification documents.

Once past the preliminary interviewing stage, you may then begin to conduct the actual interview. Your goal at this point is twofold: (1) to obtain an oral, and witnessed, admission of guilt, and (2) to obtain sufficient related information that can be used to prepare a subsequent written statement. The interview and the statement need not be lengthy or elaborate. In fact, do your best to avoid a lengthy interview. Keep in mind that any admission of guilt, oral or written, obtained by the use of intimidation, threat, coercion, or promise of any kind will be inadmissible in court and could leave you vulnerable for civil liability. You must be able to demonstrate that all such admissions are voluntary—another good reason to have a witness present.

Conduct the interview and obtain the necessary details in an orderly and logical manner. Make notes as you go along (your witness can perform this function). At the very least, you need to obtain and include in the written statement, the following information:

- The date.
- The location (city, state).
- The name and location of the store.
- The full identity and address of the shoplifter.
- The time of the offense.
- A description of each item taken, including its value.
- The method used by the shoplifter to conceal the merchandise.
- An admission that the merchandise was taken without any intention of payment.

With the interview concluded and the admission of guilt obtained, your next step is to have the shoplifter execute and sign a written statement. Figure 4.5 provides a sample of a standard statement form. Although it is desirable to have the statements in the shoplifter's own handwriting, it is not absolutely necessary. The written statement, while serving as a valid form of confession, also is an excellent vehicle for performing several other functions. In addition to including the specific issues itemized above, follow these guidelines when obtaining a written statement from a shoplifter.

FIGURE 4.5   Sample of Standard Statement Form.

STATEMENT

Date:_____   Time:_____

Location:_____

City/County of: _____ State:_____

      I, _____, state that before
I was questioned by _____
he/she identified himself/herself to me as_____
_____ .

      I hereby offer this statement, voluntarily and of my
own free will without having been subjected to any threats,
unlawful inducements, or promises of reward or immunity.

_____

_____

_____

_____

_____

_____

_____

_____

_____

_____

_____

_____

_____

_____

_____

_____

Page_1_of_3_pages

FIGURE 4.5 *(Continued)*

Statement of _____(Continued)

    A. Consent to search and recover other stolen store property.

> *"I also admit to having the following additional stolen store property:*
>
> _____
> _____
> _____
> _____
> _____
>
> *It is located at:* _____
> _____
>
> *I hereby voluntarily grant permission for _____ to enter the above described location and seize and recover all such property as described above."*

    B. Civil Release

> *"I hereby release the person or persons who detained me in connection with the aforesaid incident and his or her principals, employees and customers from any claim or demand arising out of or in connection with said incident."*

Page 2 of 3 pages

FIGURE 4.5   *(Continued)*

Statement of _____(Continued)

      I have read this entire statement which consists of _____ pages. I have initialed each page and each correction. I fully understand this statement and it is true, accurate and complete to the best of my knowledge and belief.

_____

Signature

_____

_____

_____

Address

_____

Signature of person obtaining statement

_____

_____

_____

Position and address

_____

Signature of witness

_____

_____

_____

Position and address

Page _3_ of _3_ pages

(*Source:* ProTect - Retail Loss Prevention)

- **Make sure the statement includes a paragraph attesting to the voluntary nature of the statement.** Such a paragraph can simply state:

  > I hereby offer this statement, voluntarily and of my own free will, without having been subjected to any threats, unlawful inducements, or promises of reward or immunity.

- **If applicable, obtain a Consent to Search Release.** If it is determined during the interview that the shoplifter has, in his or her automobile or home, other items stolen from the store, a comment giving permission for a search and recovery of such items should be included in the statement. A separate, voluntary Consent to Search Form can also be used (see Figure 4.6).

  Professional security officers frequently do not apprehend shoplifters until they have reached their automobiles. By delaying the apprehension, these officers have found that they were able to recover additional merchandise that had been stolen by brazen shoplifters who had made more than one trip into the store. A word of caution, however. Shoplifters frequently work in groups. Do not follow someone out to a remote parking lot where you could be attacked and severely beaten.

- **Include in the statement form a standard paragraph that absolves you and the store from civil liability charges in case an error has been made and no offense has been committed.** Or, you can use a separate form, referred to as a Civil Release, in such instances. A copy of a Civil Release is shown in Figure 4.7. Prior to using the form, you should discuss it with your personal attorney and the local Prosecuting Attorney, to ensure that the format is proper for your local area.

  If you wish to include a Civil Release paragraph in the shoplifter's statement, you can use or adapt this phraseology:

  > I hereby release the person or persons who detained me in connection with the aforesaid incident and his or her principals, employees, and customers, from any claim or demand arising out of or in connection with said incident.

FIGURE 4.6   Sample of Voluntary Consent to Search Form.

VOLUNTARY CONSENT TO SEARCH

I, _____,
have been informed of my constitutional right not to have a search made of the premises hereinafter described without a search warrant and of my right to refuse to consent to such a search.

I hereby voluntarily waive such rights without having been subjected to any threats, unlawful inducements, or promises of reward or immunity, and grant permission to
_____ and

_____

to enter and conduct a complete search of my premises located at_____

_____

(or, my vehicle, which is fully identified as follows:
_____)

The above named persons are hereby authorized to seize and recover all such stolen property as they may discover. Further, I state that I will make no claim against the above named persons, the ___(Name of business)___ ,
its officers and employees, in connection with any legal suit or demand arising as a result of this search.

_____
Signature

_____

_____
Address

Witnesses: (Name, Position, Address)

_____

_____

(*Source:* ProTect - Retail Loss Prevention)

FIGURE 4.7   Sample of Civil Release Form.

CIVIL RELEASE

I,_____,
of _____(Address)_____,
for valuable and sufficient consideration of forebearance of
Prosecution running to and received by me, do hereby
release and forever discharge individually and severally the
employees, directors, and stockholders of the _____
_____(Name of business)_____
from any and all demands, claims, or causes of action
whatsoever which I may now have, may have had, or may
have in the future by reason of, or in any matter related to
my_____(Detention, Arrest, Discharge)_____,
for _____

_____
at _____(Location)_____
on _____, and I hereby waive all right, title
and interest in property surrendered in connection with the
aforementioned charge.

_____
Signature

_____
Date

Witnesses: (Name, Position, Address)

_____
_____

_____
_____

(*Source:* ProTect - Retail Loss Prevention)

- **Make sure you have all necessary signatures.** These include:

  —The signature and address of the shoplifter.

  —Your signature, position, and address.

  —The signature, position, and address of the witness.

  In the event the shoplifter declines to sign the statement after it has been prepared, make a note on it to that effect, sign and date it, and have the witness sign it.

- **Call the police.** After the statement has been obtained, notify your local police, if they have not already been summoned, and give them all the details of the offense. As a general rule, they will take custody of the shoplifter. The person who witnessed the act of shoplifting will be required to appear before a magistrate and swear to and sign the Warrant for Arrest. Read the warrant carefully to ensure that it is correct. Never sign a blank warrant.

- **Prepare a record of the incident.** While the events are still fresh in everyone's mind, brief, written statements setting forth the entire incident should be made by everyone involved in the observation, apprehension, and interviewing of the shoplifter. Depending on the role played, these statements, including appended sketches when appropriate, should include these details of the incident:

  —The date, time, and location within the store.

  —The role and/or employment position of the witness.

  —A complete description of the shoplifter, plus those of any accomplices.

  —A description of the merchandise taken.

  —The method(s) used by the shoplifter to steal the merchandise.

  —The general pattern of the activities of the shoplifter while in the store.

  —The point of exit from the store.

  —The place of apprehension and the identity of those involved.

  —Comments made by the shoplifter at the time of the apprehension.

—Comments made by the shoplifter during the interview, with emphasis on admissions of guilt.

These statements should then be signed, dated, and filed in a safe place. They may be used to refresh memories when testimonies are given at a subsequent trial of the shoplifter.

Handling Juvenile Shoplifters

Shoplifting by juveniles poses special problems. When caught, their handling, under the law, is different from the procedures used for adults. Arrest warrants cannot be obtained against juveniles, defined, usually, as persons under 18 years of age. Instead, when criminal complaints are made against juveniles, it is done by way of a Juvenile Petition.

Each local jurisdiction has its own procedures for the handling of juveniles apprehended for shoplifting. Some police departments want to be notified of every such apprehension because they feel that, based on their information, they can assist in deciding whether prosecution of repeat offenders is warranted. Other police departments do not want to be notified unless parents are uncooperative and legal action is desired. Still others take a middle stance. They will come to the store and take the offender home to his or her parents or call the parents to the store.

Juvenile detention for shoplifting is a serious matter that you must coordinate with your own local police department. Once the procedures have been agreed on, write them down and make them a part of your store operating policies and be sure that all members of your staff are aware of them.

CARE AND CONTROL OF SHOPLIFTING EVIDENCE

Many shoplifting cases have been lost in court because the evidence— that is, the merchandise stolen—was not retained, was lost, or was improperly safeguarded. To obtain a successful shoplifting prosecution, you must be able to demonstrate that an intact *chain of custody* has existed from the time the merchandise in question was retrieved from the shoplifter until presented in court.

One of the first things to do when an individual is arrested for shoplifting is to mark the merchandise recovered. This should be done by the person who witnessed the shoplifting and who will appear as the complainant against the shoplifter in court. That person should initial and date each piece of merchandise recovered, preferably right on the merchandise itself rather than on a price tag or product tag that may be accidentally torn off.

A special Evidence Tag can be affixed to the merchandise for this purpose. Place the marked merchandise in a sealed bag or box, and have the complainant—the store employee who will represent the store in court—initial it. The bag or box should be marked to indicate the date, the name of the store, and the identity of the person apprehended. The bag or box and its contents should then be retained in a safe place until the trial. This evidence must be brought to court by the complainant. Examples of an Evidence Tag and a form that can be used to mark and identify the sealed box or bag of evidence are shown in Figure 4.8.

In many cases, the police officers who take custody of the shoplifter will also take custody of the evidence. If that is the normal procedure in your locality, make sure you obtain an itemized receipt for all of the merchandise released, and retain it in a safe place until the trial. After the trial is over, you will need the receipt to get your merchandise back.

If the police do not take the evidence, it will be up to you to safeguard it. *Do not return it to stock.*

COURT APPEARANCES

Once you (the complainant) have entered criminal charges against an individual, you will usually be required to appear in court that same day or the following morning. Rarely will you actually "go to trial" at

FIGURE 4.8 Sample of Evidence Tag and Seal for Stolen Merchandise.

EVIDENCE TAG

Description: _____

_____

Received/
Seized From: _____

_____

Received By: _____

_____

Date Obtained: _____ Time: _____

Offense: _____

_____

CHAIN OF CUSTODY

Date	From	To

Print Name _____ Print Name _____
Signature _____ Signature _____
Purpose of Transfer _____

Date	From	To

Print Name _____ Print Name _____
Signature _____ Signature _____
Purpose of Transfer _____

Date	From	To

Print Name _____ Print Name _____
Signature _____ Signature _____
Purpose of Transfer _____

FIGURE 4.8   *(Continued)*

EVIDENCE SEAL

Location: _____

Owner/Victim: _____

Name of Suspect: _____

Offense: _____

Comment: _____

_____

All evidence contained herein has been identified, initialed and recorded on Evidence Tags. I have sealed the container and have initialed the seal.

Date _____   _____

                                Signature

_____

_____

                            Position and Address

BOX/BAG ____ **of** ____.

EVIDENCE

(Source: ProTect - Retail Loss Prevention)

that time, but be prepared by bringing the evidence with you. As a general rule, you will receive, at a later date, notification or a subpoena that states the specific date and time you are to be in court.

Make sure that every witness who receives a subpoena gets to the trial. Cases have been lost and civil suits for false arrest have been initiated because complainants and witnesses failed to appear in court.

If there are unusual or extenuating circumstances in the case, it is a good idea to arrive at the court in advance of the time set for the trial and discuss the situation with the prosecuting attorney.

All testimony given in court must be accurate, impartial, nonprejudicial, and truthful.

Discussion of Shoplifting Incidents

Exercise extreme caution in discussing shoplifting incidents, especially before they are brought to trial. Casual remarks, such as "I know that he is a shoplifter" or "I know that she is a thief," could be overheard by someone known to the person about whom the remark was made and could result in a civil suit against you for defamation of character. Once a warrant has been issued charging someone with an offense, the incident should not be discussed with anyone except involved store personnel, the police, and the prosecuting attorney.

Dropping Charges

Occasionally, after formal charges have been made, mitigating circumstances are developed indicating that it would serve the best interests of all parties if the proceedings were halted, that is, if the charges were dropped. The decision to "drop charges" or *nolle prosse,* will be recommended by the prosecuting attorney. However, the decision cannot be made without your approval. Unless it is clearly warranted, you should never make such a decision without obtaining legal advice.

If you agree with the decision to drop the charges, a Civil Release form must be signed, in the presence of the prosecuting attorney, by the person arrested. This is to prevent the possibility of a civil suit being filed against you for any arrest or detention suffered by the individual as a result of the incident. This form is similar to the form shown in Figure 4.7. Retain the original of the Civil Release in a safe place.

CONCLUSION

The information presented in this chapter clearly reflects the enormous problem shoplifting is to retailers. There are numerous legal dangers, and a fine legalistic line must be walked before an apprehension and a successful prosecution for shoplifting can be made.

Your goal should be prevention, not apprehension. If you hope to have any degree of success, you must train your management and general sales staff.

In addition, you, as the store owner or manager, must meet with your local police department and prosecuting attorney and establish procedural guidelines for the apprehension, transporting, arrest, and prosecution of shoplifters. You should also become actively involved in your local merchants' associations and establish cooperative alerting programs with other retailers in your immediate operational area. Working together, you can and will make a difference.

SHOPLIFTING PREVENTION CHECKLIST

☐ Train employees to prevent shoplifting rather than watch it occur.

☐ Design the store layout in such a manner as to deter shoplifting.

☐ Arrange the fixtures in the store to provide line-of-sight coverage of potential shoplifters.

☐ Make sure all high-value merchandise is properly protected.

☐ Double-price all expensive items, with the secondary marking located in a hidden position.

☐ Use deterrent devices and systems such as locks, alarms, mirrors, and electronic sensors.

☐ Implement a "shoplifter alert" notification plan.

☐ Make sure employees are knowledgable on the various types of shoplifters and on the methods used to shoplift.

☐ Train all employees to recognize potential shoplifters. (Refer back to Figure 3.1.)

☐ Train all employees in proper antishoplifting customer relations.

☐ Train all store employees—especially store management and supervisory personnel—in proper procedures for confronting, detaining, and arresting shoplifters.

☐ Coordinate with the local police on how to arrest and transport shoplifters. Develop and implement special policies for handling juvenile shoplifters.

☐ Make sure all store managers know how to properly handle shoplifting evidence, court appearances, and dropping charges.

☐ Incorporate all shoplifting prevention policies into the store's written operational manual.

CHAPTER FIVE

Armed Robbery

Although armed robbery is one of the most potentially dangerous situations you may face as a retailer, the inherent risks, from both a personal and a financial standpoint, can be controlled.

You must understand from the onset, however, that it is foolhardy to argue with a gun. Your efforts should be directed toward controlling and reducing the occasions when you are most vulnerable to armed robberies and toward instituting procedures that will minimize your financial loss if and when you are actually robbed.

By definition, robbery is the taking of property of another by force or the threat of force. Unlike burglary, which involves breaking into a premises when no one is around, robbery is a personal, face-to-face confrontation. It is a frightening, traumatic experience.

As pointed out in Chapter 1, you should exercise extreme caution when opening and closing your store and when making bank deposits. Your risk of being held up at those times is very high. You are equally vulnerable to being the victim of an armed robbery when your store is open for business, and this chapter addresses that latter period of vulnerability.

Unless you carry high-value merchandise such as jewelry, or your store is large enough to generate large amounts of cash and thereby attract the professionals, you will most likely be confronted by "semi-professional" or "amateur" robbers. Unfortunately, they are the ones who are most dangerous. Most of them are drug addicts, juveniles, young men seeking to make a name for themselves, or mentally unstable individuals who view robbery as the only solution to their pressing financial problems. They are all nervous, desperate, and subject to going completely out of control. Treat them as you would fine china— "Handle with Care."

Accept the fact that you have no control over someone who bursts into your store brandishing a gun, and demands all of your money. You do, however, have control over certain other aspects of this crime. You can control the amount of your loss and you can institute policies that will minimize the danger of personal injury and aid in the apprehension and conviction of the perpetrator. In short, there are actions you can take before, during, and after an armed robbery that will make the best of a very unpleasant and dangerous situation.

BEFORE A ROBBERY OCCURS

Alertness, proper training, and effective cash management can minimize—and in some cases, prevent—losses caused by armed robbery.

Not only should you know what to do about armed robberies, but it is also essential that your employees receive proper training in this vital subject. Share with them all of the information in this chapter. It may save you some money, and it could save a life—perhaps yours. Educate all employees to follow these precautionary guidelines.

- Be alert to what is going on in your store and in the immediate vicinity. Watch for individuals who act suspiciously, that is, people who seem to be determining the location of employees and of closed-circuit television cameras and alarm systems. Be especially watchful if, in addition to a suspicious person inside, you can see someone else sitting outside in a vehicle. Increase your vigilance just prior to closing time, when there may be only a few customers in the store and your employees are engaged in their closeout activities. If anything doesn't seem right, do not hesitate to call your local police.

• Implement logical cash management policies. This can help decrease the financial loss suffered as the result of an armed robbery. It stands to reason that the less cash there is on hand for a robber to take, the smaller your loss will be. Do not allow large amounts of cash to accumulate in the store. Make bank deposits every day, and make partial bank deposits when warranted, especially during busy sale and holiday periods. If it is not practical or if it is unsafe for you to leave the store and make such deposits yourself, explore using the services of an armored car company.

• Instruct your cashiers and sales personnel not to let large amounts of cash accumulate in their registers. Make frequent cash "pulls" from them. This is especially important for registers located near exits, which are frequently the targets of "snatch and run" specialists. To minimize losses by opportunistic thieves, instruct your sales personnel to keep large-denomination currency under rather than in the cash drawer. When you make periodic cash pickups from a register, count the money with the salesperson responsible for it, and provide a signed receipt for the amount taken. This will help in closing out the register at the end of the business day (or shift), and it will absolve you from being considered responsible for any subsequent "shortage" reported by a dishonest cashier.

• Consider installing "drop" boxes or "slot" safes at certain register or department locations, to further safeguard excess cash. These boxes and safes, which are usually bolted to countertops and to floors and bear signs indicating employees cannot open them, are effective deterrents to robbery. If you decide to get one, make sure that it is properly made and installed. Check whether some type of baffle or mechanism behind the slot prevents dishonest employees from "fishing" for the money envelopes contained inside. Figure 5.1 gives examples of cash repositories.

FIGURE 5.1   Cash Protection Systems.

(*Source:* PERMA-VAULT Safe Corp.)

You may also want to consider the installation of a secondary, hidden repository such as a wall safe or a beneath-the-floor safe, for large amounts of money or exceptional valuables. If you believe this type of additional safe is warranted, have it installed when the store is closed and do not mention it to your general store employees.

Your robbery prevention planning should consider the installation of some of the various types of alarm and camera systems described in Chapter 3. Another type of alarm, referred to as a "money trap," is available for use in cash registers and money drawers. It is designed somewhat like a clip: when the money is pulled out of it, an alarm is activated. Figure 5.2 is a photograph of this type of device.

The use of "bait money"—packets of paper currency of which the serial numbers have been recorded or in which explosive vials of indelible inks have been placed—may also be considered if you regularly have large amounts of cash on hand, as, for example, in an office or a cashier's cage.

FIGURE 5.2   Wireless Money Trap.

(*Source:* Linear)

DURING A ROBBERY

This is a dangerous time. If at all possible, you, as the store manager, should try to take the lead in communicating with the robber. If a relationship, adversarial as it may be, can be established between you and the robber, the others present in the store—other employees and customers alike—become incidental players and are much less likely to be harmed. Such action on your part will greatly help in defusing the highly charged and hazardous initial period of confrontation when the robber is trying to establish control.

Try to remain calm and obey the commands of the robber. Remain still and instruct all others to do the same. Cooperate, but only to the extent necessary. Do not, for example, remove cash from or volunteer the existence and location of any secondary or concealed money repositories.

If a note is presented, do not give it back unless it is asked for. Drop it in the register or safe or set it aside. The fingerprints and writing on it could be valuable evidence for the police.

The best thing you can do during a robbery is to be observant. Detailed physical descriptions, including the manner of dress, are among the most important items of information you can furnish the police. As soon as possible after the robbery, write down your description of the robber(s). Have all other witnesses do the same. Insist that they write down their descriptions separately, without comparing notes. The descriptions should include:

- General physical characteristics—sex, race, age, height, weight, and stature—with special notation of any disabilities or of any scars, marks, or tattoos.
- Hair (color, length, style).
- Face (shape, complexion, mustache, beard, glasses).
- Voice (high, low, accent, speech impediment).
- Names, if more than one robber and they addressed each other by name.

- Hands (rough, smooth, rings, wristwatch, gloves).
- Clothing (describe fully, top to bottom, hat or mask to shoes).
- Weapons (type, color, where concealed).

An example of a standard Incident Report Form suitable for descriptive purposes is shown in Figure 5.3.

If possible, without endangering yourself or anyone else, attempt to determine the robber's direction and manner of escape. If a vehicle was used, try to obtain as much descriptive data regarding it as you can.

AFTER A ROBBERY

Unless someone was able to activate a silent holdup alarm or was able to surreptitiously make a telephone call while the robbery was in progress, *the first thing you must do is call the police.* You will probably speak to a dispatcher who will, in turn, relay your information to a patrol car. *Stay on the line until all of the necessary information is transmitted.* If in the excitement of the moment you hang up too soon, the police may be delayed in getting to your store or, worse, they may unknowingly pass the escaping robbers while en route to your store because, in your haste, you hung up before passing on to the police a description of the robber's vehicle.

While waiting for the police to arrive, protect anything the robber may have touched—the cash register, the countertop, or merchandise. All may bear latent fingerprints of the robber. If shots were fired and shell casings were ejected, leave them right where they fell. Your best course of action is to get the rope or clothesline from your emergency kit and cordon off the entire area until the police arrive and complete their investigation.

FIGURE 5.3   Sample Form for Reporting a Robbery.

INCIDENT REPORT FORM

Date and Time of Incident: _____

Location of Incident: _____

Type of Incident: _____

Report Made By: _____

Brief Narrative of Incident

_____
_____
_____

Description of Suspect(s) (Use separate form for each)

General: Sex_____, Race_____, Age_____, Height_____, Weight_____

Scars/Marks_____, Other _____

Hair: Color_____, Length _____, Style _____

Face: Type_____, Complexion _____, Mustache/Beard _____

Voice: Pitch_____, Accent_____, Impediment_____

Clothing: Describe - top to bottom _____
_____
_____

Mask: Type_____, Color _____

Weapon: Describe - Gun_____, Knife _____
_____

Names: Unknown_____, Known_____

Call other suspects by name: _____

Items Taken

Money: Amount Bills_____, Amount Coins_____, Other _____

Total Monetary Loss:_____

Merchandise: Description and Value (Use reverse if necessary)_____
_____

Manner of Escape

On Foot_____, By Vehicle_____, Other_____

Vehicle Description: Make_____, Color_____, Type_____, Year_____

Tag No. _____, Condition_____

Direction of Escape: _____

_____
Signature

(*Source:* ProTect - Retail Loss Prevention)

ARMED ROBBERY PREVENTION CHECKLIST

☐ Follow effective cash management procedures to minimize the amount of loss caused by an armed robbery.

☐ Make sure your cash management procedures include frequent withdrawals of funds from the cash registers or the use of drop boxes or slot safes.

☐ Install and use a secondary, hidden safe.

☐ Take special safety precautions when opening and closing the store. (Refer back to Chapter 1.)

☐ Instruct all employees as to what they should do in the event of an armed robbery.

☐ Incorporate these policies and procedures for preventing armed robbery into the store's written operational manual.

CHAPTER SIX

Fraud

CHECK FRAUD

Except for relatively small convenience purchases, most retail transactions today are carried out via the use of credit cards and checks. There has been a tremendous increase in credit card payments, but checks still play a significant role in the retail business environment. Once viewed as a convenience for customers, and frequently only grudgingly allowed, payment by check has now become a "right," and woe to the merchant who refuses to accept one. Indeed, for a number of reasons, many retailers today probably could not survive if they discontinued accepting checks.

Checks have some good points. They encourage sales and minimize the store's vulnerability to theft and robbery by reducing the amount of cash on hand. Unfortunately, they have one major, significant weakness. Just because you have a check in hand does not mean you have the money that it represents. A third party is involved—the bank on which the check was written. Unless the bank accepts the check as a valid negotiable instrument—the check "clears"—you wind up with nothing. To make matters worse, you suffer a double whammy: (1) you've lost your profit on the sale, and (2) you've lost the merchandise that was carried away by the bad-check passer. It's no wonder one sees "In God We Trust—All Others Pay Cash!" posted on the walls of small businesses across the country.

Trying to determine which checks are good and which are bad is like trying to pick out the shoplifters from among all of the honest, legitimate customers who enter your store. Like shoplifting, you will not be able to completely eliminate the problem, but there are certain things you can look for and actions you can take to minimize your losses.

Types of Checks

Although a wide variety of checks have evolved to service the financial and commercial communities, only a few of them are regularly encountered in the retail environment. They are:

- **Personal checks** written and signed by the individuals presenting them and drawn against deposits in their own bank accounts.

- **Payroll checks** issued by an employer to a specifically named employee.

- **Government checks** issued by various federal, state, or local government agencies for a wide variety of entitlement, tax refund, pension, or salary purposes.

- **Two-party checks** written by one party, the individual against whose bank account the check is drawn, and made payable to a second party who, in turn, endorses it to a third party who finally presents it for cash.

- **Travelers' checks** sold in preprinted denominations by large firms such as American Express to people, usually tourists and business travelers, who do not want to carry large amounts of cash. The traveler signs the check at the time of purchase and countersigns it when it is presented for payment.

- **Certified checks** issued by banks. They bear on their face the bank's guarantee of the availability of the funds and the validity of the signature.

- **Money orders, postal and others.** Although technically not checks, money orders are often used in the same kinds of transactions. Because they are issued for specific amounts, they are rarely used to make retail purchases. Some merchants will accept them, however, especially when presented to cover previously written bad checks or to make payments on open accounts.

Bad Checks Defined

Bad checks, that is, those refused by banks for payment, are of two clearly defined types: (1) those presented by persons who make no attempt to hide their identity and (2) those presented by persons who do not give their correct name. The first type of bad check is generally returned by the bank with the notation "Nonsufficient Funds" (NSF) or "Account Closed" (AC), which usually means that the customer has overdrawn the account, inadvertently or otherwise. These checks can often be redeposited after contacting the customer or the bank and determining that sufficient funds have been made available. The second type, presented by persons who attempt to hide their true identities, are usually returned by banks with the notations "Forged," "Stolen," or "No Account." These checks are most likely to result in significant losses to the retailer.

Check Acceptance Guidelines

The only effective course of action you can take to minimize bad-check losses is to develop and implement precautionary check acceptance guidelines. Figure 6.1 provides guidelines that all employees should follow. Post these guidelines in the back of the store or in the Employee Lounge.

Check Verification Services

If you are concerned about accepting a check for a big-ticket item, you may be able to obtain a verification of the account and the availability of funds by contacting the issuing bank. Some banks, however, will only perform this service for depositors.

FIGURE 6.1   Guidelines for Accepting or Rejecting Checks.

- Restrict the approval of check acceptance to trained supervisory personnel.
- Accept personal checks for the amount of purchase only. Travelers' checks cannot be held to this rule, but be cautious about accepting large-denomination travelers' checks for small purchases.
- Limit, insofar as possible, your acceptance of checks to those drawn on banks within your trading area.
- Examine carefully each check presented. *Insist that it be written and signed in your presence.* Pay particular attention to the following:
  - **Legibility.** Do not accept checks that are not written legibly. They should be written and signed in ink and should not have any written-over amounts or erasures.
  - **The date.** Do not accept checks that are undated, postdated, or more than 30 days old.
  - **The amount.** Make sure that the check is written for the amount of the purchase and that the numerical and written amounts agree. Set a limit on the amount of purchase you will allow by check.
  - **The bank location.** Make certain the check reflects the name, branch, city, and state location of the bank on which it is drawn.
  - **The presenter's identification.** The check should have imprinted on it the name and address of the presenter.
- With the check in hand, require at least two pieces of documentation to corroborate the customer's stated identity. Keep in mind, however, that if the check is stolen so also may be the identification presented. **Ask for identification that bears a laminated photograph or physical description and the signature of the bearer.** Some forms of identification are much better than others. For example:

(Continued)

FIGURE 6.1   *(Continued)*

- Do not accept as identification easily obtained or easy-to-forge documents such as social security cards, business cards, library cards, and insurance cards.

- Accept, after close examination and comparison, cards that bear laminated photographs, physical descriptions, and/or signatures: drivers' licenses; government, military, and employer identification cards; major credit cards and shopping plates that carry both an account number and a signature element.

- Pay special attention to a comparison of the signatures. Be especially wary if, when filling out the check, the individual seems ill at ease, tries to distract you, or seems to be slow and unusually meticulous in signing his or her name.

- If you become suspicious and have any inkling of fraud, attempt to stall the suspect and call the police immediately. If you are unsuccessful in detaining the suspect until the police arrive, get a good description of the suspect and any accomplices involved plus, if possible, a description of any vehicle used and the direction of departure.

- If you approve the transaction by check, do one more thing to prevent another type of check-related loss. Before handling the receipt to the customer, write on the back "Paid by Check" and the date, and initial it. Some individuals knowingly write bad checks and come back to the store, before the check has had time to clear the bank, to ask for cash refunds. When successful, they wind up with your money. This safeguard must be emphasized to the personnel in your store who accept checks and those who handle refunds.

If your check trade is sufficiently large and your losses have become significant, you would be well advised to consider signing up with one of the many commercial check verification services that are now available to retailers. These high-technology systems, developed initially to stem credit card fraud, have expanded to include check fraud as well. With massive data banks, these electronic systems make verifications by comparing account numbers, cross-checking addresses, and accessing national lists of stolen checks and bad-check passers. Before contracting with such a firm, however, make sure that it operates in compliance with the Fair Credit Reporting Act.

You may also want to consider granting check cashing cards to your regular customers. These cards can be issued after the customers' application information has been checked by an appropriate credit agency.

At the very least, maintain a list of bad-check passers who have victimized you in the past. The list can be expanded through cooperative exchanges of data with other store owners or your local merchants associations.

Collections and Prosecutions

After you have been notified by your bank that a deposited check is "bad," your course of action, although limited, is quite clearly defined. It will depend to a great degree, at least initially, on the stated reason for nonacceptance and the type of check involved. If, for example, the check in question is a personal check returned for "Nonsufficient Funds," your focus will be directed toward "making it good," that is, collecting the money. If, on the other hand, it is returned as "No Account," "Closed Account," or "Forgery," you probably have only one recourse: seek criminal prosecution.

Collections

Unless your business is located in a high-crime area (in which case, you probably won't be accepting many checks anyway), or your customer base is highly transient because your business is located in a major tourist area or along an interstate highway, most of the bad checks you get are likely to be caused by nonsufficient funds. With some effort on your part, most of these checks are collectible. The same holds true, but to a lesser extent, for checks returned because of closed or nonexistent accounts. Prompt action on your part is required, however. Do not procrastinate. This is not a time to be concerned about alienating or embarrassing a customer.

When a check is returned because of nonsufficient funds, contact the customer, notify him or her of the stated reason for the return, and inform him or her that unless the check is redeemed in person immediately, you will redeposit it; further, if it is returned a second time, you will have no alternative but to take other legal action. *Do not accept another personal check as payment.* People offering to make this kind of restitution are usually only attempting to buy more time.

If this course of action proves unsuccessful or you are unable to contact the customer, you will have to initiate collection action. The first thing you should do is send the customer a notice of the returned check via registered mail, return receipt requested. This is the so-called "5-day letter" (or "10-day letter," depending on your local jurisdiction) that must be sent before a merchant can initiate criminal prosecution. The notice should be accompanied by a copy of the check and a summary of your state's laws regarding the passage of bad checks.

A sample of a 5-day letter is shown in Figure 6.2. Before imitating it, however, you should contact your attorney, your local police department check-fraud unit, or your prosecuting attorney's office for assistance in implementing the proper format and phraseology for your area.

As a final collection method, you might ask your servicing bank to put the check on "collection" status. Your bank will then return the check to the issuer's bank and, when sufficient funds are deposited in the issuer's account (if one exists), the check will receive priority payment.

If the above action is unsuccessful, the registered notice brings no response, and follow-up telephone calls prove useless, you can, as a last resort, turn the matter over to a collection agency. Be prepared,

**FIGURE 6.2   Sample of "5-Day Letter" Form for
Collecting on Bad Checks.**

5-DAY LETTER

Date: _____

To: _____
        _____
        _____
        _____

     We hereby give you notice that Check No._____,
dated the _____ day of _____, 19_____,
drawn by you on the _____
bank of ____(State)_____, and payable to the order of
_____,
in the amount of _____ dollars,
has been dishonored by nonpayment.

     Unless the amount due thereon, together with inter-
est and protest fees (if any), is paid to the holder within 5
days after receipt of this notice, such legal action as may be
necessary will be taken.

                              _____
                              Company Name

                              _____
                              Name of Official

                              _____
                              _____
                              _____
                              _____
                              Position and Address

(*Source:* ProTect)

however, to share with the agency a significant percentage of any funds collected. Beyond those actions, your only recourse is to seek criminal prosecution.

Prosecutions

After all collection efforts have failed, you may then take your registered letter receipt—or the letter itself, if it has been returned to you as undeliverable—and the check in question to the check-fraud unit of your local police department and initiate prosecution proceedings.

Bear in mind that the check is your evidence. Take good care of it. Place it in a sealed envelope, and handle it as little as possible. Make every effort to identify the writer of the check and connect him or her with the receiving of specific merchandise from your store. A good practice is to have the person who approves the check initial it, date it, and note on it a brief description of the item purchased. This association refresher can be an asset when preparing for or giving courtroom testimony.

If the police decide to pursue the prosecution, you will be asked to complete certain forms that must be approved by the check issuer's bank. A warrant for the issuer's arrest will then be issued. *Once a warrant has been issued, do not, under any circumstances, allow the issuer of the check to "make it good."* Such a decision can only be made by the prosecuting attorney or the judge hearing the case.

If the police determine that the amount of the check does not justify the expenditure of their resources, your only recourse will be to have your attorney file a civil complaint. A subpoena will then be issued and a court date set.

CREDIT CARD FRAUD

The use of credit cards, in all their various forms and as issued by banks, department stores, oil companies, and other private organizations, is central to the successful operation of today's retail establishment. With over one billion cards in use, the potential for increased sales is enormous. Unfortunately, so also is the potential for fraud.

Unlike check fraud, however, credit card fraud is not viewed by the average retailer as a major problem. If the credit transaction is handled properly, any subsequent financial loss will be absorbed by the card issuing firm, not the retailer—a significant difference from the total loss that could be suffered if that same retailer is stuck with a bad check. Such an outlook may be understandable, but it is somewhat out of focus. The millions of dollars lost by credit card issuers because of fraud is recouped from all of us in the form of higher annual fees and interest rates. In other words, credit card fraud affects everyone, retailers and consumers alike.

Types of Credit Card Fraud

There are known to be major criminal credit card laundering operations, but the average retailer is most likely to be confronted by two types of credit card fraud: (1) the use of a stolen credit card or (2) the use of an altered or counterfeit card. Merchants who accept charge sales by phone or mail are subject to a third type of fraud; individuals may search trash bins for carbon-paper inserts or copies of completed credit sales forms and use the identity and numbers noted thereon to make illegal purchases.

The use of stolen credit cards, or the opportunistic misuse of lost cards, is usually the province of individuals operating alone; the use of altered or counterfeit cards is a sign of organized criminal rings. Often connected to widespread criminal affiliations and marked by high levels of technical competence, these rings threaten the very existence of many credit card issuing agencies. The most common forms of the rings' activities involve the reembossing of account numbers, the altering of signature panels, and the counterfeiting of the magnetic strips. Altered cards are almost impossible to detect.

Industry Safeguards

Trying to keep one step ahead of criminals is a never-ending task for credit card issuers. New technology to produce a tamper-proof card is constantly being tested and implemented. Among the safeguards currently in use are holograms, three-dimensional pictures that are imbedded into the face of the cards and are extremely difficult to reproduce. Other safeguards include the use of photographs of card holders, indent printing on the signature panel, and multiple-card validation codes.

Most new safeguards require the merchant to use point-of-sale computer-terminal verification systems. Electronic verification systems are currently used to process over 75 percent of all credit card transactions. The systems are very effective, but they do not relieve the retailer of all responsibility.

Merchant Responsibilities

The payment of customer charges by credit card issuing agencies is neither automatic nor guaranteed. Payment will not be made if the retailer fails to process the charge sale properly. It is important, therefore, for all sales personnel handling charge sales to be aware of the procedures listed in Figure 6.3. Post these guidelines in the rear of the store or in the Employee Lounge.

COUNTERFEIT CURRENCY

Rapid technological advances in photographic, printing, and reproduction equipment have caused tremendous increases in counterfeiting and are forcing nations worldwide to redesign their currency and institute improved anticounterfeiting measures into their engraving and printing processes. The development and eventual introduction of such new currency is currently under way in the United States, but full implementation is still several years away. In the interim, retailers will continue to be subjected to losses resulting from the acceptance of counterfeit currency.

As a general rule, the counterfeit will be first detected by your bank, in one of your deposits. The bill will be confiscated and your account debited accordingly. To reduce such losses, you must institute proper cash handling procedures and provide your sales personnel

FIGURE 6.3   Procedures for Evaluating Credit Cards.

- Credit cards are the property of the issuing companies and may be recalled at their discretion. When one is presented to make a purchase, the salesperson should retain possession of it until the verification process has been completed and the authorization granted.
- Closely examine the credit card presented. Make sure that the expiration date has not passed.
- If your store is not equipped with a terminal that electronically "reads" the face of the card and verifies its valid use before processing the purchase, check the card number against the card recovery bulletins and "stop lists" provided by the card issuer.
- Do not exceed established floor limits without obtaining authorization.
- Use the proper form for the charge card presented.
- Ensure that all copies of the transaction slip are legible.
- Make sure the sales slip is signed in your presence. Be especially wary if the purchaser seems ill at ease, tries to distract you, or is slow or unusually meticulous in signing his or her name.
- *Compare the customer's signature on the sales slip with the signature on the card. They must match.* This is the single most important check that can be made to detect fraudulent use of credit cards.
- If the charge card has not been signed, or if the signatures on the card and on the sales slip do not match, ask for additional identification that bears a photograph, physical description, and signature.
- Be suspicious of cardholders who make multiple purchases, all under the floor limit, or who rush in, select merchandise rapidly, and keep the amount under the floor limit.

(Continued)

FIGURE 6.3 *(Continued)*

- If you suspect fraud, attempt to stall the suspect and call the police immediately. If you are unsuccessful in detaining the individual until the police arrive, get a good description of the suspect, any accomplices involved, and, if possible, any vehicle used and the direction of departure.

with effective counterfeit detection methods. The guidelines listed in Figure 6.4 should help.

If your detection efforts succeed and you believe that someone is attempting to pass a counterfeit bill in your store, hold on to it, do not give it back. Hang on to your merchandise also. Call the police or the U.S. Secret Service, which has investigative jurisdiction over the counterfeiting of U.S. currency. If the bill-passer cannot be detained, try to get a good description of the suspect, any accomplices involved, and, if possible, any vehicle used and the direction of departure. Do not surrender the bill to anyone but the police or Secret Service agents.

Not everyone who passes a counterfeit bill is a counterfeiter. Most bogus currency is passed along by totally innocent people who have received it in change somewhere else and have not realized its counterfeit origin. Be careful in making any unwarranted or unjustified accusations.

FAST-CHANGE AND CON ARTISTS

One will take your money by trick and sleight-of-hand, and the other will talk you out of it: fast-change and con artists are birds-of-a-feather—vultures who prey on the naive, the inattentive, and the untrained. With their exceptionally fertile imaginations and innovative ruses, these smooth-talking hustlers are responsible for millions of dollars of losses suffered by the retail community every year. Unfortunately, most of the store owners victimized don't even realize what has happened; they attribute most register shortages, instead, to simple cashier errors.

FIGURE 6.4   Guidelines for Identifying Counterfeit Currency.

- The best method of detecting a counterfeit bill is to compare it with a genuine note of the same denomination. This is easier to do if all cash registers are kept orderly, with all bills segregated by denomination, face up and in the same direction.

- Look for differences, not similarities. Pay particular attention to the characteristics of the paper and to the quality of the printing.

- Keep in mind that genuine currency is printed on special paper that has imbedded in it tiny red and blue fibers that are visible to the naked eye and can even be picked off the paper if first loosened. Counterfeiters attempt to duplicate these fibers by using a separate printing process. Close examination will reveal that they are surface-printed and are not the randomly dispersed and imbedded fibers found in genuine notes.

- Watch out for currency that looks "washed out." The production of genuine currency requires not only the skills of master engravers, but the use of specially designed and very expensive printing equipment, both usually beyond the means of most counterfeiters. As a result counterfeit notes frequently look "washed out" and flat.

- Look for details. Most counterfeit currency lacks fine detail, especially in the area of the portrait. On a genuine note, the lines in the portrait background form distinct squares; on the counterfeit, many of these squares may be filled in.

- Examine the Treasury seal and the Federal Reserve seal for comparative purposes. On a genuine note, the sawtooth points surrounding these seals are clear and distinct; on the counterfeit, they are frequently blurred and ragged.

- Check the serial numbers. On good bills, they are evenly spaced and aligned; on counterfeits, they often are not.

To have any hope of thwarting the efforts of these slick criminals, it is imperative that everyone who handles sales transactions be knowledgeable about the basic tactics they use and stay constantly alert for their appearance.

Fast-Change Artists

These individuals are the magicians of the group. With a constant stream of comments, questions, and distracting chatter, accompanied by rapid currency manipulations and exchanges, these fast-change artists can literally make your money disappear. They are exceptionally adept at confusing inexperienced cashiers during the change-making phase of sales transactions. Some act very friendly and sincere; others express indignation and outrage and are verbally abusive. However, they all have the same purpose in mind—to separate you from your money.

A subclassification of the fast-change artist is the currency switcher. Technically, currency switchers commit a form of counterfeiting: they employ the use of altered paper notes, which they usually attempt to pass by using some of the same chatter-and-distract tactics as the fast-change artist. These individuals will take, for example, a number of twenty-dollar bills, cut or tear one numerical value corner from each of them (they will still be negotiable) and then paste these corners on a lower denomination bill. After some smoothing out, sanding and color blending, these "raised" bills are then passed to busy cashiers in the hope that the alteration will not be noticed. If it is, they simply protest that the bill was given to them in change at some other location. They will try to take it back and will angrily exit the store . . . to try the ruse someplace else.

Cashiers' comparison of the face of bills should include a matchup of the portrait and symbols, not just the numbers at the corners.

Con Artists

True con artists are award-worthy actors who relieve you of your money by first gaining your *con*fidence (hence the term con artists) with convincing and often elaborate ruses. The term con artist is used to describe some individuals who engage in various check, credit card, exchange, and refund schemes, but the persons we are concerned with here are the purists—the calculating, innovative, imaginative confidence men and women who prey on your point-of-sale operations.

An example of a con artist ploy was given in Scenario 3 of this book's Introduction, where I described how "flashers," impersonating U.S. Secret Service agents, can walk away with "counterfeit" currency because of their elaborate, convincing, and successful scheme.

The number of cons that have been used successfully would provide enough material for a separate book. No sooner does one ploy become overused and played-out, when another is developed to take its place. Some tactics have become classics and, with a different cast of characters and ingenious adaptations, seem to go on forever. Here is one of those classics.

Classic Con Artist Ruse

A young teenager gets on a checkout line that has been specifically selected because it is busy and is staffed by a young, apparently inexperienced cashier. The teenager makes a small purchase, pays for it with a twenty-dollar bill, takes the change and merchandise, and exits the store.

Further back in the line, two or three people behind the teenager, is an elderly woman dressed in rather old, frayed clothing. When it is her turn at the register, the woman purchases several small items and pays for them with a five-dollar bill. After receiving her change and while the cashier is bagging the merchandise, the woman pauses, rummages through her purse, gets a very concerned look on her face, and, in a quavering voice, says to the cashier, "I'm afraid you made a mistake; I gave you a twenty-dollar bill and this is only change for a five." The clerk replies, "I don't think so, ma'am; I'm quite sure you only gave me a five."

At this point, the con kicks in. The woman starts to sob and then, in a loud, emotional voice, begins to relate a sympathy-engendering story about being in line at the welfare office earlier in the day and having run into an old friend there. Wanting to jot down the new telephone number of the friend and not having any other paper handy, she wrote the number on the only twenty-dollar bill she had in her possession. Setting the hook, the woman states, "That has to be the twenty-dollar bill I gave you. You just look in your register. The number written on it is 415-6785. You just look in your twenties. I'm sure you'll find it."

The cashier, by now taken in by the woman's situation and sincerity, begins to believe that perhaps a mistake was, in fact, made. She opens the register and lo and behold! there is the twenty-dollar bill with the telephone number on it, just as the woman predicted. By this time, people are gathering around and the line is backing up. The cashier, now perhaps completely flustered, takes out the twenty-dollar bill, apologizes profusely to the woman, and either hands her the bill or gives her fifteen dollars to supplement the change from the five-dollar bill. The old woman, dabbing at her eyes, puts the profit from the con in her purse and exits the store.

She then goes out into the parking lot, joins the teenager (actually, her grandson), and together they drive off to find their next victim. Her grandson-accomplice had dropped off the marked bill and she got back at least fifteen dollars' profit—or maybe even *your* twenty dollars. This con could have been prevented.

Preventive Measures

Minimizing losses caused by fast-change and con artists is relatively simple. It begins (there is no end) by making everyone aware of the problem, by stressing constant vigilance, and by implementing some basic cash-handling safeguards. Make sure your employees follow the procedures in Figure 6.5.

Instruct all cash-handling personnel to check their gullibility at the door when reporting for work. They must be trained and constantly vigilant about the existence of con artists. They should question the stories told to them by "customers" who attempt to separate them from their (your) money.

FIGURE 6.5   Guidelines for Thwarting Con Artists.

- Closely examine all money received from customers, to see that it has not been altered or does not appear to be counterfeit.

- Never place the customer's money into the register drawer immediately upon receipt; instead, place it in a safe and open spot and leave it there until the proper change has been counted out, given to the customer, and the sale concluded.

- Count the change for transactions twice, once to yourself and again as you give it to the customer.

- Of prime importance, close the register drawer immediately and call for the manager or a supervisor if any customer questions the amount of change given or attempts to confuse you in any way. The manager or supervisor can then, in the presence of the customer, check or otherwise take a reading of the register and resolve the problem.

The "Hostage" Con

Before concluding this section on con games, one more should be mentioned; the "hostage" con. Most other cons are relatively painless, except for the ache in your wallet, but the hostage con is usually a very stressful and traumatic experience. Like most cons, it has various adaptations, but it usually works something like this.

While working in your store one evening, you get a telephone call. Responding, you hear a gruff voice state, "I know you are Mr. Wilson of 2705 Cloverdale Lane. We are holding your wife and daughter hostage. Do as you are told and no one will get hurt. If you don't you will never see them again. Your every move is being observed. Place five thousand dollars, in small bills, in a small box outside your rear door. Do it within five minutes and don't call the police, and everything will be OK. Once we have the money, your wife and daughter will be released. You can talk to them in about 30 minutes. Don't call before then. Move!"

If you are like most store owners, you gather the money, place it outside as you were told, and pray that no harm comes to your family. Thirty minutes later, you call home and discover that your wife and daughter have spent the evening working on costumes for the school play. By the time the police are called, the money is long gone. Too bad; that would have been an excellent time to have activated a silent holdup alarm.

At this point, you can do little besides alerting your business associates and organizations in an attempt to prevent others from being similarly victimized.

CONTROLLING FRAUD BY DISHONEST VENDORS

Depending on your type of business, some of your losses may be attributable to dishonest vendors-deliverers, route-personnel, and manufacturers' representatives. Sadly, this is especially true if the same individual services your store over a long period of time, and a friendly, trusting association develops. Store personnel will then tend to lower their guard, which affords the dishonest vendor numerous opportunities to engage in "short" deliveries and outright theft. Another possibility is the development of a close relationship between a vendor and an employee and their subsequent collusion to commit illegal acts. Alertness on your part, plus adherence to a few simple guidelines, can greatly reduce your vulnerability. For example:

- Assign an experienced and trustworthy employee to handle all deliveries to your store.
- Count all incoming boxes and cartons, and frequently perform random spot-checks of the contents for extra verification and to prevent bill padding.
- Do not leave merchandise unattended on receiving docks.
- Do not allow vendors to enter your stockrooms unaccompanied.

- Make accurate counts of cartons containing "returns," and frequently look inside them to check for concealed merchandise.

- Pay special attention to any boxes or cartons that the vendor may be removing from the store. This is a very common method that dishonest vendors and store employees use to collusively steal from the store merchandise that they plan to split between them.

- When possible, rotate the duties of store personnel assigned to check-in of vendors, to discourage collusion.

- Be watchful for and become suspicious of any of your employees who seem to spend inordinate amounts of time outside at a vendor's truck, especially if the receiving area is somewhat secluded or is located near the employee parking lot. Payoffs, in the form of a case or two of merchandise in return for allowing the vendor to make a "short" shipment or engage in bill padding, are frequently made to dishonest employees in this manner, especially during holiday periods.

EXCHANGE AND REFUND FRAUD

Every purchase made does not, unfortunately, result in 100 percent customer satisfaction. Some items purchased are subsequently found to be too big, too small, the wrong size, or the wrong item entirely. Sometimes, people just change their minds about a purchase they have made. To promote customer satisfaction and store loyalty, retailers must have a policy to handle such situations. Many stores, however, have such lax policies, if they have any at all, that they are completely at the mercy of thieves who specialize in fraudulent exchange and refund schemes. Some of the more common schemes are as follows:

- Opportunists search trash bins or pick up discarded sales receipts near the front of the store or around cash registers, and then select items in the store with equivalent prices and turn them in for refunds.

- Shoplifters brazenly bring back stolen merchandise for cash refunds.

- Con artists, such as the paint man mentioned in scenario 5 of the Introduction, engage in a wide variety of refund ruses.

- Eagle-eyed comparison shoppers purchase an item at a discounted price and then return it at a store that sells the same item but at a higher price.

- Salvage buyers obtain damaged goods at greatly reduced prices and then attempt to either exchange or return them at another store for full price.

- Bad-check passers purchase items with a check they know is no good and then, before the check has had time to clear the banking system, try to return the merchandise for a cash refund.

Taking your cues from these tactics, it is not difficult to determine what you must do to control the losses that could result. For example:

- Establish one specific location within the store for handling returns and exchanges; staff it with an experienced employee.

- If possible, locate your return and exchange section close to the entrance to the store.

- Place signs prohibiting customers with refunds and exchanges from entering the main body of the store unless they check in first at the refund desk or (if you do not have such a dedicated section) with the checkout cashier. Such a practice will greatly stem your losses from ploys like the paint man's and from refund scam artists who pick up discarded receipts, take equivalent-value merchandise off the shelves, and then ask for refunds.

- If at all possible, and if you can do it without alienating your regular customers, institute a stringent policy of no exchanges or returns without a valid receipt.

- Insist that the merchandise returned be in salable condition unless it contains defects resulting from poor product quality or manufacture. To preclude being stung by salvage buyers, do not take back any damaged merchandise unless it is accompanied by a valid receipt from your store.

- Establish specified time limits beyond which customers cannot return merchandise, to prevent being victimized by persons who purchase bulk quantities of out-of-date merchandise and attempt to return them for credit or refund at the full price.

- Use preprinted forms for returns, to record the full name, address, and telephone number of the customer making the return. Record also the identity of the item and its price, and have the customer sign the form. An example of such a return/exchange form is shown in Figure 6.6.

- Post all of the conditions of your return and exchange policies at appropriate locations within the store.

FIGURE 6.6   Sample Form for Accepting Returned or Exchanged Merchandise.

RETURN/EXCHANGE FORM

Description of Item: _____

Date Purchased: _____ **Receipt: Yes**_____**No** _____

Merchandise: Cost_____ **Tax**_____ **Total**_____

Reason for Return/Exchange: _____

TO BE COMPLETED BY CUSTOMER ONLY

Name: _____

Address:_____

City: _____ **State:** _____ **Zip:** _____

Tel No: _____

Customer Signature:_____

Signature of Refund Clerk: _____

Signature of Supervisor: _____

Attach Customer's Receipt

(*Source:* ProTect - Retail Loss Prevention)

One additional scheme relating to refunds must be mentioned. It relates to losses caused by insiders—your own employees. The number of employees who have been caught engaging in dishonest refund schemes is amazing. Then again, maybe it isn't amazing, because all a dishonest refund clerk has to do is pick up a receipt, if one is even required, fill out a form using any name listed in the local telephone book, put it and the receipt in the register and pocket the cash equivalent.

To prevent such blatant theft, you, as the store owner, must exercise careful control over the entire refund and exchange operation. Determine the average volume of refunds so that any increase from the norm will be immediately noted. Maintain a written log. If you notice an unusual pattern, attempt to narrow the time period down to a specific employee, and increase your vigilance. Check for the merchandise that was ostensibly returned.

The best check is to take a number of the return forms, which show the names, addresses, and telephone numbers of the customers who supposedly made the returns, and call them or write to them. You can, in all sincerity, couch your conversation or letter to state that the contact is for the purpose of seeking customer satisfaction. Be aware that some recipients may be partners of your dishonest employee. But sooner or later, if an employee is engaged in a refund scheme, you are going to have someone tell you that they have never returned an item to your store. Bingo! You just caught a thief.

There is an easier way to prevent this type of employee dishonesty. Institute, and communicate to all employees right from the onset, your policy of contacting a representative number of customers who make returns. Such action on your part will not only prove to be an effective deterrent to theft, but will be looked on most favorably by your customers.

FRAUD PREVENTION CHECKLIST

Check Fraud Prevention

☐ Develop and put into practice effective check acceptance guidelines. (Refer back to Figure 6.1.)

☐ Make sure all store management personnel are knowledgeable about proper collection procedures. (Refer back to Figure 6.2.)

☐ Make sure all store management personnel are knowledgeable about proper prosecution procedures.

Credit Card Fraud Prevention

☐ Make all personnel aware of the various types of credit card fraud.

☐ Develop and implement proper credit card acceptance policies. (Refer back to Figure 6.3 for guidelines.)

☐ Use credit card recovery bulletins and "stop lists," if these capacities are not available in your cash register terminals.

☐ Establish a floor limit for credit card charges.

☐ Emphasize to all employees that sales slips must be signed in their presence and that signatures must match those on the credit cards presented.

☐ Instruct all employees as to what they should do if they suspect fraud.

☐ Use an electronic verification and authorization system.

Counterfeit Currency Prevention

☐ Train all cash-handling personnel in how to detect counterfeit currency.

☐ Instruct all employees as to what they should do if they suspect an attempt is being made to pass counterfeit currency.

(Continued)

Preventing Fraud by Fast-Change and Con Artists

☐ Train all employees in how to identify and recognize methods used by fast-change and con artists.

☐ Train all employees regarding proper cash-handling procedures.

☐ Implement a fast-change and con artist alerting system among local retailers.

Controlling Fraud by Dishonest Vendors

☐ Make store management and all employees aware of the various methods vendors can use to pad bills, make "short" deliveries, and steal merchandise.

☐ Establish firm policies regarding the actions of vendors.

☐ Alert store management to the possibility of illegal collusive acts between vendors and store employees.

☐ Rotate the store personnel assigned to check in vendors, as a way of discouraging collusion.

☐ Make frequent spot-checks of both vendor deliveries and returns.

Preventing Exchange and Refund Fraud

☐ Train all employees to recognize the wide variety of exchange and refund scams.

☐ Develop a store policy and effective procedural guidelines for handling refunds and exchanges.

☐ Make sure store management utilizes and closely monitors these procedures.

☐ Post signs stating the store's refund policy.

☐ Designate one specific location within the store for handling all returns and exchanges.

(Continued)

(Continued)

☐ Staff the exchange/refund desk with an experienced employee.

☐ If possible, locate the exchange/refund desk near the entrance to the store.

☐ Make sure the sales floor and the area around the cash registers are kept clear of all discarded receipts, to preclude their being used fraudulently.

☐ Implement special procedures, including the use of specifically designed forms and the contacting of customers, to deter and detect refund fraud by store employees.

PART THREE

Internal Loss Prevention

This part pertains to losses caused by internal forces—your employees. This is an unsettling and distasteful topic because it focuses on your own store "family," your associates and coworkers, who may have become your close friends and with whom you frequently spend more time than you do with your natural family. As painful, and as truly regrettable as it may be, however, *the average retailer suffers more losses because of the dishonest acts of his or her own employees than are suffered as a result of all external forces put together.* To any store owner, this is a very disquieting and sobering thought.

Fortunately, this is the one aspect of an effective loss prevention program where you can exercise the most control. Before you can establish effective controls, however, you need to identify your vulnerabilities. This means knowing the various methods that employees use to steal both money and merchandise.

Effective preemployment practices, sound employee relations programs, and well-designed internal controls procedures can help you in
detecting—and, in fact, preventing—many employee theft problems
before they even get started. This part covers a wide range of significant internal loss prevention issues, and is designed to assist you in
your efforts.

CHAPTER SEVEN

Hiring
Trustworthy Employees

E mployee problems are management problems. More precisely, problems of employee dishonesty are problems that are directly attributable to lax or nonexistent supervisory control. Policies and procedures need to be developed and implemented that will safeguard the monetary and inventory assets of the store and, at the same time, aid in the rapid detection of dishonest acts and the identity of the employee(s) involved. These policies begin with effective prescreening of prospective employees and continue through implementation of appropriate control procedures that govern all vulnerable facets of the operation of the store.

A caring and friendly but, nevertheless, businesslike atmosphere must be maintained, and a climate of honest endeavor must be established. All of those characteristics begin with you, the store owner or manager. If you are observed by employees taking merchandise out of the store without payment, or dipping into the cash register for a few dollars, you send an exceptionally bad signal. Your highly questionable activities not only foster a lack of respect, but are clearly indicative of an absence of accountability that frequently tempts employees to do likewise.

It's your store. Control it and run it right. If you don't, the odds are that you will not be running it very long.

A key factor to the continued success of almost any business is the presence of a dedicated, knowledgeable, well-trained, and honest work force. However, such a staff doesn't just materialize; it must be created and then sustained. It requires planning, formal policies and procedures, and constant supervisory oversight. This is especially true in instilling and maintaining employee integrity.

Every retailer who has to hire a work force to conduct the business should have formal, written policies governing employees' activities. The policies need not be elaborate, but they should focus on and clearly state the procedures for conducting the significant operational activities of the store. They should also spell out the consequences of any violations of those policies. Having preexisting guidelines that are made known to your employees at the time of hire will simplify any subsequent terminations for cause and ease potentially contentious situations.

Subsequent sections of this chapter cover a number of employee-related loss prevention concerns that, depending on your size and operational environment, you may wish to incorporate into your own formal policy documentation.

The formulation of company policies is governed by the size and nature of the business and by the operational and managerial philosophy of the store owner. There are, however, certain commonalities applicable to all retail establishments.

As you prepare your policies, pay particular attention to personnel, merchandise, monetary, and operational controls. The Internal Loss Prevention Checklist, at the end of this chapter, can help you quickly identify issues of concern that should be addressed in your policy directive.

In addition, consider the following checklist of significant control issues that you may want to include in your procedural guidelines:

- A clear statement that the penalty for theft is termination.

- Prohibitions regarding the falsification of time and attendance records or the signing-in or signing-out of another employee.

- Prohibitions regarding an employee's working under the influence of or possessing alcohol or drugs on company property.

- Prohibitions regarding fighting, horseplay, gambling, or engaging in sexual misconduct on company property.

- Prohibitions regarding the deliberate destruction, damage, or misuse of company property or that of another employee.

- Prohibitions regarding hazardous work habits that jeopardizes the safety of coworkers or customers.

PREHIRE SCREENINGS

Acquiring the services of a reliable, knowledgeable, and trustworthy employee starts with the application process.

The Application Form

Require all candidates for employment to complete a preprinted application form. If you do not already have one, standardized forms can be obtained from most large stationery and office supply firms, or you can create your own. At the very least, it should contain blocks for providing the following information:

- The full name of the applicant and space to include any other names by which the applicant is known.

- A chronological listing of addresses for at least the past five years.

- Education history—the names and locations of schools attended, the dates of attendance, and the dates and types of degrees obtained.

- Employment history—the names of the companies worked for, the inclusive dates of employment, the positions held, the names and telephone numbers of immediate supervisors, and the reasons for leaving.

- A listing (name, address, telephone number, and position) of at least three business references.

- A listing (name, address, telephone number, and position) of at least three personal references.

- A space for noting, in localities where the query is permitted, any convictions (not arrests).

The form should contain a statement that (1) certifies that all of the information provided is true, (2) gives you, the employer, permission to conduct any additional credit, police, or background checks that may be required, and (3) releases you from any claims or events that might result as a consequence of such checks. The form should be signed and dated by the applicant. An example of an application form is shown in Figure 7.1.

A word of caution is in order, regarding the employment application form you use. During the past several years, a number of federal and state laws have been enacted that severely limit the questions an employer can ask of a prospective employee. Known generally as equal employment opportunity and privacy legislation, these laws impose strong penalties for violations. For example, in addition to the well-known restrictions on inquiries relating to an applicant's sex, age, religion, or national origin, the following lines of inquiry are prohibited:

- Marital status.
- Family composition, and any inquiries as to who will take care of the children while a parent–applicant is at work.
- The identity of persons who live with the applicant.
- Whether the applicant rents or owns a residence.
- Whether the applicant's wages have ever been garnished.
- Whether the applicant has ever been arrested.

Before adopting any employment application form for your use, have it reviewed by an attorney who is well versed in the labor relations field, to ensure that you do not inadvertently violate any hiring laws.

FIGURE 7.1   Sample Employment Application Form.

APPLICATION FOR EMPLOYMENT

Position Applied For: _ _____

Name (*Last, First, Middle*): _____

Address: _____

_____

Tel. No: _____ Social Security No: _____

Are you legally eligible to work in the United States?   Yes _____ No _____

Do you have any relatives employed at this company? Yes _____ No _____

  If yes, state name and position: _____

Do you have any physical, mental, or medical impairment that would interfere with your ability to perform the job for which you are applying? Yes _____ No _____

> NOTE: All prospective employees must submit proof of identity and eligibility for employment prior to appointment. A social security card and drivers license are preferred.

RESIDENCES (*For past five years*)

From	To	Address

EDUCATION

Highest grade completed: _____

Degrees (*with dates*) or credits earned: _____

Honors/Awards: _____

From	To	School Name	Location

Special qualifications and skills : _____

_____

(Continued)

FIGURE 7.1 *(Continued)*

Application for Employment (Continued)

EMPLOYMENT HISTORY *(Give in chronological order beginning with current or most recent position. Include military service and volunteer experience. Additional experience may be listed by adding separate sheets or a personal resume.)*

Employer: _____ From:_____ To: _____
Address: _____
Job Title: _____ Salary Start_____ End_____
Supervisor: _____ Telephone No. _____
Describe Duties: _____
_____
_____

Reason for Leaving: _____

Employer: _____ From:_____ To: _____
Address: _____
Job Title: _____ Salary Start_____ End_____
Supervisor: _____ Telephone No. _____
Describe Duties: _____
_____
_____

Reason for Leaving: _____

Employer: _____ From:_____ To: _____
Address: _____
Job Title: _____ Salary Start_____ End_____
Supervisor: _____ Telephone No. _____
Describe Duties: _____
_____
_____

Reason for Leaving: _____

Employer: _____ From:_____ To: _____
Address: _____
Job Title: _____ Salary Start_____ End_____
Supervisor: _____ Telephone No. _____
Describe Duties: _____
_____
_____

Reason for Leaving: _____

Page 2 of 3 pages

FIGURE 7.1   *(Continued)*

Application forEmployment (Continued)

PROFESSIONAL REFERENCES *(List three persons who are NOT related to you and who have definite knowledge of your qualifications and fitness for the position for which you are applying. Do not repeat names of supervisors given above.)*

Name	Address	Tel No.

PERSONAL REFERENCES *(List three persons who are NOT related to you who can attest to your honesty, integrity and good character.)*

Name	Address	Tel No.

CRIMINAL RECORD

Have you ever been convicted of any offense against the law? Include convictions by general court martial while in the military service. Omit juvenile offenses and minor traffic violations. Yes _____ No _____ If Yes, give date, place, charge, court, and fine or sentence.

_____

_____

STATEMENT BY APPLICANT

I certify that all of the statements made in this application are true and complete to the best of my knowledge. I understand that a false or incomplete answer may be grounds for not employing me, or for dismissing me after I have begun work.

I hereby authorize you to make such inquiries of my education, employment, financial and such other related matters as may be necessary to make an employment decision. I further release all such persons and entities from all liability that may arise as a result of responses they may provide in connectiion with my application.

Signature of applicant _____ Date _____

This application must be signed.

Page 3 of 3 pages

(Source: ProTect - Retail Loss Prevention)

Bear in mind that these laws relate not only to the application form, but also to verbal inquiries made of an applicant during the personal interview phase of the employment process. Because these laws are in a constant state of flux, make it a point to check periodically with your attorney for new changes that may affect your personnel practices.

The Initial Interview

When the applicant has completed the form, you should ask to see at least two pieces of identification that will corroborate the personal data given. With the form in hand, you should then review it and interview the applicant. At this stage, you are looking for any unexplained gaps in the applicant's residential, education, and employment histories. If the chronologies listed do not account for all periods of time, it may mean that the applicant was in prison or is attempting to hide some other unfavorable incident such as a firing at a previous place of employment. Continue until you are satisfied that everything has been covered. If all of the other information appears correct and your assessment of the applicant's personal traits and job qualifications is favorable, your next step is to verify everything listed on the form and what was told to you during the interview. Inform the applicant of this procedural requirement and terminate the interview.

The Background Investigation

Do not, under any circumstances, hire someone without making any background checks. You may get away with it a few times if you are lucky, but, eventually, you are going to get burned. Not only may you be bringing into your employ a criminal or someone who only wants the job so that he or she may later embezzle funds or pass off merchandise to friends and relatives, but you may also be victimized by any of a number of "new employee" schemes.

In one of the most common schemes, a neat, well-dressed young man enters your store and applies for a job, in response to a "Help Wanted" sign in the window. He fills out an application and it looks good. The subsequent interview also goes very well—so well, in fact, that, to fill your pressing vacancy, you offer him immediate employment. He accepts and starts to work. Several hours later, before the end of his shift, he complains of not feeling well and asks if he can go out to his car to get some medication. Sure. He goes out but never returns. Thinking that he may be very sick and in need of some assistance, you go out to check on him. He is gone, and so is his car. And so is all the money, *your* money, that was in his register plus as much valuable merchandise as he could stuff into his pockets.

A background check should include, at a minimum, police and credit checks and contacts with the applicant's former employers. Places of residence and education should also be verified and references should be interviewed. If you do not have the time to do this yourself, or if you feel incapable of or uncomfortable about handling the background check, any number of reputable investigative agencies will, for a fee, conduct background investigations for you.

If at all possible, conduct the background checks yourself, even if you have to do it telephonically or by correspondence. Pay particular attention to verifications and information received from the applicant's references.

The following guidelines should help you conduct a thorough background check:

- **Talk to the applicant's former employers.** In addition to being useful sources for verifying the identity, work record, and residence history of applicants, contacts with former employers can provide much other useful information. Unfortunately, however, because they are concerned about possibly violating some provision of the privacy legislation or of being sued for slander or libel, many companies now only release a minimum amount of information regarding former employees. Contact with an applicant's former employers, however, is still your best source of useful information.

  If possible, talk to the applicant's former immediate supervisors. Try to ascertain character and work-ethic information. Determine why the applicant left. Was the applicant laid off? Fired? Did he or she resign? Or was he or she allowed to resign in lieu of termination? Why? Get as many details as possible. One key question should always be asked: "Would you be willing to hire _____(name)_____ again?"

- **Get professional references.** These are not to be confused with former employers or supervisors. Professional references are sometimes coworkers, but more often are others in the professional community who have knowledge of the applicant's qualifications for the position you are seeking to fill. In addition to probing for work qualification information, attempt to develop character assessment information plus residence and prior employment histories of the applicant. As a general rule, you will find that these individuals are much more willing to provide information about an applicant than can be obtained from official company sources. Determine the length of time they have known the applicant and the nature of the association. Ask, specifically, whether they recommend the applicant.

- **Check character references.** Don't neglect to contact and interview the character references provided by your applicant. An amazing number of people list as references prominent individuals who are pillars of the community but, alas, have never heard of the applicant. Check each reference. If your applicant has resorted to such a ploy, his or her integrity is obviously questionable.

- **Check education.** Verify all attendance and degrees claimed by the applicant. If appropriate for the existing vacancy, have the applicant bring in a copy of his or her official transcript. Contacting former teachers and guidance counselors is often very productive.

- **Check financial status.** The best way to determine the applicant's financial history is to make an inquiry at your local credit bureau. In most localities, you will need the applicant's written consent before such an inquiry will be conducted. Such checks are highly desirable because they will often reflect the degree of financial pressure currently facing the applicant. Such pressure, unfortunately, is often an indicator that the applicant may be susceptible to a temptation to steal from the business.

- **Ask about a criminal record.** Knowledge of whether an applicant has been convicted of a theft-related or other serious crime is a significant factor when you are considering an individual for employment in your store. In many localities, applicants can be requested to bring in a document from the local police department reflecting their criminal history, if any. Arrests are not generally listed nor are they usually releasable; an arrest is not a conviction and does not signify guilt. Many people are arrested, but not all are found guilty of the crime with which they have been charged. Don't confuse the two.

  Restrictions on the release of criminal record information vary from jurisdiction to jurisdiction. Determine what your local rules are, and do your best to obtain the criminal history of everyone you hire.

- **Check residence history.** As you conduct your checking of former employment, record the applicant's residence history. Are there any residences that the applicant did not list on the application? Contacts with former landlords can reveal evidence of the applicant's financial integrity. Has the applicant ever been evicted from a place of residence? If so, attempt to determine why. Pay attention to any gaps in the applicant's residence chronology. Cross-check it with the employment history. If all the pieces don't fit, you may be looking at a potentially serious problem. Where was the applicant? In prison? What is he or she trying to hide?

- **Verify employment history.** Be especially wary if your checking develops information that the applicant has worked at other places in addition to those listed on the application form. Why were they omitted? Is the applicant attempting to hide a termination? If possible, contact the former employer and obtain the details.

The Evaluation

When you have completed the verification checks and have obtained, from other sources, as much information about the applicant as you can, check the data against the facts provided you by the applicant. If there are significant discrepancies and obvious gaps in employment and residence histories, you will have to either eliminate the applicant from consideration or conduct another interview to resolve all outstanding issues. If you opt for the latter and can subsequently obtain sufficient information from the applicant to alleviate all your concerns, you may then make the offer of employment. Before doing so, however, doublecheck all explanations offered by the applicant that do not ring true.

NEW EMPLOYEE BRIEFINGS

After the background checks have been completed and are considered to be favorable, your next steps are to make a formal employment offer and, if accepted, to conduct the new employee briefing. Do not conduct this briefing in a casual or cavalier manner. It is your single, best opportunity to impress on a new employee your security and loss prevention policies.

At this point, your written policies, whether in the form of a handbook or in some separate documentary format, come into play. Ideally, you should provide each employee with a personal copy of these policies, but the important point is to have something available that each new employee can read.

After all questionable policy issues, if any, have been clarified, have a separate document available for the employee to sign, acknowledging an awareness and an understanding of them. Figure 7.2 provides a sample form.

Make two copies of the signed document. Give a copy to your new employee and retain the original in your store's personnel files. As previously mentioned, preexisting guidelines that are made known to and are acknowledged by employees in writing at the time they are hired, simplify any subsequent terminations for cause and ease contentious situations.

FIGURE 7.2   Sample of Acknowledgment of Company
                        Policies Form.

ACKNOWLEDGMENT OF COMPANY POLICIES

I, _____
hereby acknowledge I have been informed that, as a condition of employment, I will be expected to know and abide by
all company policies, rules and procedures.

I hereby state that I have been furnished with a copy
of all such policies and have received clarification and explanation of all those that were not clear to me. I now fully
understand and will abide by all of them.

I recognize that my failure to abide by any of these
rules could result in my immediate termination.

I hereby acknowledge receipt of this document and
understand that the original will be retained in my company
personnel file.

_____
Signature

_____
_____
Address

_____
Date

_____
Witness

_____
Position

(*Source:* ProTect - Retail Loss Prevention)

EMPLOYEE HIRING CHECKLIST

☐ Develop a formal, written policy governing the activities of employees.

☐ Require all applicants for employment to complete a preprinted application form.

☐ Establish a formal prehire screening process.

☐ Subject all applicants to a background investigation.

☐ Give all new employees a formal briefing regarding company policies.

☐ Require all new employees to sign a document acknowledging awareness and understanding of company policies.

☐ Make sure store management knows how to identify a "high-risk" employee and puts this knowledge into practice.

CHAPTER EIGHT

Preventing Theft by Employees

Throughout this book, I have given a number of warnings and admonitions regarding employee theft. Among those mentioned were the dishonest assistant manager who reenters the store, after closing, to remove merchandise; employees who throw merchandise in trash bins for retrieval later or out of windows to waiting accomplices; and sales personnel who "slide" merchandise to their friends, take part in collusive acts with vendors, or engage in fraudulent refund schemes.

Unfortunately, these examples are just the tip of the iceberg. Employees, like shoplifters and con artists, have very fertile imaginations and can dream up countless ways to separate you from your money and your merchandise. If there is the need and the temptation, all the dishonest employee then lacks is the opportunity. If, because of poor controls or lax supervision, the opportunity presents itself, you are going to suffer major losses.

In addition to the methods already mentioned, here are some of the more common ways in which employees steal merchandise and embezzle funds:

- **Simple theft.** Frequently and improperly minimized by referring to it as pilferage or "toting," this type of theft relates to the removal from the store of merchandise concealed in pockets, purses, and various bags and containers.

- **Collusive theft.** Merchandise is removed by two or more employees working together—for example, a sales clerk and a janitor. The term also refers to thefts caused by employees working in concert with outsiders, such as vendors and trash collectors.

- **Product substitution theft.** Employees (or shoplifters) may remove expensive merchandise by placing it in a box from a less expensive product. Collusion with outsiders is usually involved.

- **Employee purchase theft.** They may take more merchandise than was actually paid for.

- **Inventory theft.** Deliberate "short counting" of merchandise may cover a current or previous theft.

- **Shipping and receiving theft.** In this type of theft of merchandise, employees may act alone or in collusion with others. Carton or item counts are falsified and the merchandise is stolen.

- **Sales personnel embezzlement.** Cash register operations are usually involved. Sales are underrecorded or not recorded at all, and the equivalent amount of money is taken; or, false errors and voids are claimed, and the cash equivalents are removed from the register. False refund schemes are also included in this category.

- **Accountant/Bookkeeper embezzlement.** A wide variety of schemes relate to cash reports, the accountability of funds, and bank deposits. Figures are manipulated, money is taken from register receipts that have been turned in, and bank deposits are deliberately shorted. Also, receipts for payouts made to vendors are raised, and fraudulent receipts for store expense items are created. Thefts from petty cash accounts are accomplished, usually by the alteration or creation of fictitious vouchers.

- **Managerial embezzlement.** These schemes are similar to those employed by dishonest accountants and bookkeepers, but the amounts stolen are larger and the theft frequently involves the creation of "dummy" suppliers and "ghost" employees.

FACTORS CONTRIBUTING TO EMPLOYEE DISHONESTY

Criminologists and sociologists conduct endless studies and engage in heated debates as to why some people engage in dishonest acts and others do not. Actual case studies of retail employee crime tend to reflect that three significant factors collectively contribute to employee dishonesty: (1) the need, (2) the temptation, and (3) the opportunity.

The need, in most cases, is actual or perceived financial desperation brought on, for example, by the loss of a full-time job, emergency medical expenses, unexpected automotive repairs, or other personal misfortune. The need for more money could also be symptomatic of someone who is a gambler, an alcoholic, or a drug user. Need can also be defined as desire. An example of desire as a motivating factor can be found in the young, part-time sales clerk who desires friendship and wants to stimulate her popularity with her schoolmates. To achieve her goal, she undercharges or does not even ring up the purchases they make in her department.

The temptation factor is subtler and much more insidious. It relates not only to the analogy of placing the "fox in the henhouse," but also to the development of a mental attitude within the employee that culminates in a perceived justification for committing the dishonest act. A prime example is the employee who steals because, rightly or wrongly, he or she feels underpaid, unappreciated, or treated unfairly.

The final factor, the opportunity, does not require any further definition. If there is a need and a perceived justification, all a misguided or dishonest employee requires is an opportunity and your merchandise or your money is gone. You have very little control over the need and the temptation, but you have enormous control over the opportunity. *If you can establish sufficient internal controls, you can significantly reduce the opportunities for employees to steal. The establishment of such controls, however, is only half the battle; you must implement and enforce them.*

IDENTIFYING HIGH-RISK EMPLOYEES

To develop an effective, dedicated, and honest work force, you must get to know your people. You must treat them fairly and equitably, and be attuned to their personal problems and concerns. When employees are emotionally upset and distraught because of outside circumstances, their performance will obviously suffer, which, in turn, could have an adverse effect on your business. Be sympathetic and understanding, and help them when you can. Not only is it the humanitarian thing to do, but your concern will be repaid a hundredfold in superior job performance, enhanced employee loyalty, and, most importantly, trustworthiness.

In addition, your interest will enable you to spot those individuals who are at risk—the ones whose personal affairs, life-styles, and habits identify them as being susceptible to going astray, to becoming dishonest employees. Pay particular attention to the following alerting signals:

- Significant indebtedness.
- Questionable associates.
- Excessive drinking.
- Excessive gambling.
- Drug addiction.
- Living beyond means (pay particular attention to places of residence and type of vehicles driven).
- Personality changes.

- Marital/Partnership problems.
- Unusual or secretive work habits (First to arrive, last to leave, no vacations, etc.).
- Frequent prolonged visits by the same customers.
- Abnormal relationships with vendors.
- And, especially, the disgruntled, unhappy employee.

INTERNAL CONTROL PROCEDURES

The prevention of losses caused by employees is a multifaceted problem. The establishment of certain controls is absolutely necessary, but a realistic balance must be maintained to prevent the creation of an oppressive environment in which every employee feels suspect. An overly aggressive, heavy-handed approach will only alienate your employees and make it very difficult for you to enlist their cooperation in combating all of the other loss prevention issues that must be addressed.

The following internal control suggestions, augmenting those mentioned in earlier chapters, are presented for your review and judicious implementation.

Personnel Controls

These controls relate primarily to the nonsale or nonduty movements and activities of your employees.

- **Accounting for employee time.** Time is money. To control your payroll, employees should be required to use time cards or some other written method of sign-in and sign-out accountability. Work habits should be monitored to prevent misuse of time. Magazines and newspapers visible at workstations are graphic indicators of such misuse.
- **Entry and exit.** All employees should be required to enter and exit through a specifically designated entryway or door. This

location should be monitored, especially during shift changes and at closing, by a security guard (if one is employed) or by a supervisor.

- **Employee parking.** Insofar as possible, prohibit employees from parking their private vehicles near side or rear doors and near shipping and receiving docks.

- **Employee packages.** Employees should be discouraged from bringing packages into the store. Any packages carried to work should be surrendered to store management upon entry, securely sealed, and retained in a controlled or locked repository where they are held until the employee finishes work for the day and is ready to exit the store.

- **Purses and outer garments.** Do not allow employees to take their purses and outer garments such as raincoats and overcoats into their work areas. Make every effort to provide a separate cloak room equipped with individual lockers and located in an area that can be monitored by store management.

- **Employee purchases.** This topic is of special importance. When uncontrolled, purchase is one of the major avenues used by employees to steal. *Insist that all employee purchases be transacted through store management.* Designate certain time periods when such purchases will be accepted. If purchases are made during a period of time when the employee is still on duty, the merchandise, properly bagged and sealed, should be retained by the store manager until the employee gets off duty and is ready to exit the store. There should never be a time when you, as the store manager, do not know what an employee is carrying out of the store.

Merchandise Controls

Merchandise is the lifeblood of any retail establishment. Without it, there can be no business. It must be protected from damage, misuse, and theft. Previous chapters covered the threats from outsiders. This section focuses on the establishment of controls to prevent losses caused by employees.

- **Inventories.** Periodic inventories are an absolute must. When conducted by your own staff, they should, whenever possible, be performed on a cross-department basis. If you allow employees to inventory their own departments, you are offering them a way to cover up their own thefts. The use of independent, outside inventory firms on a regular basis is also recommended.

- **Stockrooms.** Access to stockrooms should be restricted, and high-value merchandise should be protected by locks and alarm systems that are controlled by supervisors. Merchandise should be stacked neatly, to prevent damage and to make it easier to spot missing items.

- **Damaged merchandise.** Prohibit or severely limit reduced-price sale of distressed or marred merchandise to employees. This rule will deter them from deliberately damaging salable items.

- **Use of stock.** Employees should not be allowed to indiscriminately take merchandise from the sales floor or stockrooms to use for store upkeep, repair, or maintenance. The use of such materials should be first approved by store management and then recorded and accounted for as a separate class of store expenditures.

- **Out-of-area merchandise.** Store managers should keep an eye out for any merchandise found away from its designated area or department. There is usually a simple explanation, but when merchandise is found behind the counter of a salesperson, it could also mean that the employee is getting ready to steal it or pass it off to a friend.

Managers should routinely check trash bins and garbage containers for concealed merchandise. Dishonest employees, especially janitors, frequently remove merchandise from the store for later recovery from outside receptacles and dumpsters. Doubling-back after closing for the night, and then returning to drive around behind the store to check on these dumpsters can often be an illuminating experience. Employees can frequently be caught red-handed going through the trash to recover merchandise they have stolen.

Warehousing Controls

Although technically allied to merchandise controls, warehousing (receiving, shipping, and transporting) operations are of special concern and warrant independent treatment. If your business is large or is part of a chain-store operation receiving stock from a central warehouse, or if you have separate, dedicated shipping and receiving departments, you face a major loss prevention control problem. Unless closely monitored, your warehousing departments can become cancerous and, in time, cause the demise of your entire operation. No business can long exist if more merchandise is being stolen out the back door by employees than is being carried out the front door by customers.

Thefts in this category are almost always collusive. They are frequently "cross-over" thefts involving nonemployees. However, because, more often than not, they hinge on the dishonest actions of employees, this overall subject is treated here as an internal loss prevention issue.

Emphasis is on the larger, central-warehouse operations used by multiunit businesses, but the vulnerabilities identified and the loss prevention controls recommended have many applications to smaller, independent businesses as well. For example, many retailers who sell large, bulky items such as appliances, lawn and garden equipment, and hardware items, often maintain satellite warehouses and separate shipping and transportation systems to make deliveries to customers. Each of these operations is susceptible to major theft and must be controlled.

From a loss prevention standpoint, warehouse operations are essentially inventory operations. A certain amount of merchandise is received, stored or warehoused, and then shipped out at a later date. A record is maintained of everything that comes in and a record is maintained of everything that goes out. Sounds simple enough. Keeping track of everything should be no big problem, right? Wrong! Maintaining control over the merchandise in a warehouse is an exceptionally difficult task.

Warehouses, with rare exceptions, are usually chaotic environments. They are large, noisy, open-to-the-weather buildings peopled by a constant stream of individuals operating fork-lifts, carts, and motorized pallets as they move case after case of merchandise from one place to another. Some of it comes in, some goes out, and a lot of it just seems to go around and around on the tow-cart and conveyor systems forever. There are hiding places galore.

Not only is the environment inside the warehouse chaotic, the loading docks are frequently the same way. With several trucks all being off-loaded or loaded at the same time, often with noncompany drivers all clamoring for attention and priority handling, supervisors are hard put to maintain order, let alone watch for thefts.

As difficult as it may be, however, warehouse operations must be controlled. A few procedures, rigidly enforced, can make a world of difference. The following suggestions should help:

- Install bright lighting both inside and outside the warehouse. Place special emphasis on the loading dock area. Use nonbreakable light fixtures or protect them with screening to prevent their being broken by stones or pellet guns.

- Install alarm systems. In addition to your primary off-hours alarm system, install secondary open-hours alarm systems on all remote fire, emergency, and other access doors.

- Securely lock all windows that do not have to be opened. Protect them and all other openings, such as vents, with steel bars and heavy-gauge wire screening.

- Install a closed-circuit television monitoring system. Provide overlapping coverage for the loading dock area and for areas where high-value merchandise is stored.

- Install convex mirrors both for safety purposes and to aid in monitoring employee and nonemployee actions. Again, emphasize the loading dock area.

- Make sure the loading dock is well-lighted. When possible, install lights, cameras, and mirrors in positions that will enable supervisors to see into the interior of trucks as they are being off-loaded or loaded. Mobile lighting systems that can be moved from dock to dock as needed work very well. These installations will effectively deter a lot of the box break-ins and thefts of merchandise that occur in these locations.

- Do not allow employees to park their personal vehicles near the loading docks.

- Control the hours when the doors to the loading docks are open. Do not open them before normal work hours, and close them if there is a shutdown during lunch breaks.

- Stagger break periods so that some employees are on hand at all times. If that is not possible, do not allow merchandise to be left unattended on the dock during break and lunch periods.

- Discourage close association between truck drivers and loaders. Segregate the drivers' waiting area from the employees' break area.

- Do not allow truck drivers, especially noncompany drivers, to roam around the warehouse. Have a strict written and posted policy regarding this prohibition, and make it known to all incoming drivers.

- When possible, separate the receiving docks from the shipping docks.

Receiving Operations

This is where the accountability of merchandise begins. All too often, unfortunately, it is also where it ends. *Accurate records regarding the amount of merchandise received are an absolute must.* Inventories are impossible without this information. You will never be able to detect shortages unless you know what you are supposed to have on hand. Whether you own a warehouse operation or an individual store, you must have effective control of your receiving department. The following points are offered for your consideration and, depending on your operational environment, implementation as part of your company policies:

- If possible, permit receiving operations to be conducted only at certain specified times.

- Have the docking bays configured so that trucks butt up flush with the dock and warehouse wall, leaving no room for cases of merchandise to be dropped off under or around the side of a truck.

- Make sure incoming merchandise is accurately counted.

- Make occasional spot-checks of cartons, to detect thefts by drivers and off-loaders.

- Make sure supervisory personnel also conduct occasional spot-checks of incoming merchandise to ensure that the delivery driver and the receiving clerk are not engaged in a collusive "short count" scheme.

- Instruct receiving clerks to check that the right type of merchandise is being received and an inferior product has not been substituted.

- Develop procedures for handling overshipments. If there is no formal procedure, it will be easy for the receiving clerk to simply steal the merchandise or have it taken off the property by a cooperative truck driver.

- Consider the occasional use of a "blind" receiving system. Normally, when merchandise is shipped, the sending firm will forward two or more copies of the purchase order and the shipping invoice to the receiving warehouse office or store. These documents will usually reflect the case count and number of items shipped and will be used by the receiving clerk to "check-off" the shipment as it is received. In a "blind" system, the identity of the items is noted but the case count and number of items to be received is not divulged. The receiving clerk is then forced to make an accurate count of the merchandise as it is received. This count is compared with the documents in the possession of the warehouse supervisor or store owner, which indicate the actual quantities shipped. Significant discrepancies call for an immediate investigation.

- Consider deliberately "shorting" or "overing" a shipment, particularly between company locations, as an integrity check, to see whether employees will report the discrepancy.

- Be watchful for a dishonest driver who will surreptitiously reload merchandise onto a truck after it has been counted and checked off by the receiving clerk.

- Keep an eye out also for a driver who has a couple of cases of merchandise in the cab of the truck. This is usually an indication that the driver has detected a sloppy receiving operation and hopes to get away with some deliverable goods. Check out the merchandise and who the recipient is supposed to be. In split shipments, with part of the load destined for another company, you may have detected a driver theft operation. A call to the trucking company headquarters may be warranted—and well received.

- Do not neglect to count in returns received from company stores. Thefts can easily occur on both ends of the operation, at the warehouse and at the store. If it becomes known that accurate counts of returns are not being made, dishonest warehouse employees can simply take the merchandise knowing that the shortage will never be detected. At the store end, if it is known that accurate counts are not being made at the warehouse, the employee shipping the merchandise can easily "short" the return and steal the rest of it.

Shipping Operations

Uncontrolled shipping operations have been the direct cause of many business bankruptcies. Almost everything mentioned in the discussion of receiving operations, especially as pertains to loading dock controls, also applies, in reverse, to shipping operations. Instead of focusing on what is coming in, efforts are directed toward controlling what is going out.

Shipping operations entail a broader risk factor than receiving. Most receiving theft is blatant and perpetrated right at the off-loading dock. Shipping theft is often carefully hidden in a maze of fraudulent sales receipts, invoices, and delivery documents. Although direct thefts from shipping departments and loading docks is indeed common, the most insidious and dangerous thefts occur far away from those locations. For example, unless such actions are carefully controlled, a dishonest salesperson can prepare a fraudulent sales receipt for a large item, such as a refrigerator, and send it, along with the pertinent "customer" delivery data, to the shipping department. Upon receipt of the shipping order, the refrigerator is pulled from stock at the warehouse and delivered—to a friend working with the dishonest salesperson. Next week, they're going to get a washer and dryer.

If that isn't bad enough, think about the damage that can (and has been) wrought by organized gangs of dishonest sales, shipping, warehouse, and delivery personnel, all working together. Thousands upon thousands of dollars' worth of merchandise can be stolen in very short periods of time. No business, regardless of size, can long survive such onslaughts.

The control of shipping operations is a major subject to address in the development of an overall loss prevention program. Procedural guidelines to monitor shipping operations are, for the most part, self-evident. The following points are offered for your consideration:

- Every document that is used to authorize, move, or ship merchandise should be sequentially numbered *and accounted for.*

- Additional supervisory authorization should be required for the shipment of high-value merchandise.

- Frequent spot-checks of merchandise being loaded for delivery should be performed, to ensure that valid sales receipts or purchase orders exist.

- Insofar as possible, the duties of personnel assigned to shipping duties should be rotated periodically, to discourage collusion.

In addition to the losses caused by fraudulent documentation and outright cargo theft, many businesses suffer from other types of improper and illegal shipping schemes that are often overlooked. For example:

- Misuse of company mailing facilities. If the business frequently mails packages and orders to customers, the system, unless controlled, is ripe for misuse by employees, especially during the Christmas holiday season. Besides being a channel for sending personal mail and packages, the company mail system, if uncontrolled, can become a means to easily get stolen merchandise off the premises.

- Misuse of company postage meters and meters furnished by commercial package delivery service companies. Unless these meters are carefully controlled and locked up at the end of the business day, they could be improperly used and result in a significant business loss.

Transportation Operations

The movement of cargo from one place to another is carried out in a wide variety of ways—by ship, by freight train, by airplane, by truck, and by a wide number of other conveyances suitable to the locale and the product being delivered. The most common and universal carrier is the truck, and we will focus our attention on this method of transport.

Cargo shipments made by truck are transported in both common-carrier commercial trucks and company-owned trucks. You can exercise only a limited number of controls over common-carrier trucks, but you can implement a wide number of controls to prevent cargo losses from company vehicles.

Cargo theft from trucks generally occurs in four different places: (1) at the shipping dock; (2) at the receiving dock; (3) while loaded and parked in the warehouse yard; and (4) while in transit. The vulnerabilities and procedures to effectively control shipping and receiving operations have already been covered. This section will therefore address only those concerns that relate to the prevention of thefts from trucks while they are in the warehouse yard or in transit.

Warehouse Yard and Staging Area Operations

Trucks are frequently loaded in advance and then parked in warehouse yards and staging areas to await assigned drivers and subsequent delivery of the merchandise to specific stores. Unless properly safe-guarded, such loaded trucks make tempting targets for thieves. This vulnerability is significantly increased if the warehouse is not a 24-hour operation and shuts down for the night. The following recommendations should help in controlling this problem:

- If the operation is large enough, make sure the staging area, as well as the entire warehouse complex, is well lighted and is enclosed by secure, alarmed fencing.

- Use only one gate to the complex and staff it by security guards stationed in a guardhouse that is equipped with communications and rest room facilities.

- Make sure one guard remains at the gate to control traffic; another should function as a roving patrol.

- Once loaded, make sure all trucks and cargo trailers are locked with high-security padlocks, the keys to which are in the possession of and controlled by the shipping department supervisor.

- As an additional precaution against theft, make sure all loaded trucks are parked with their cargo access doors flush up against walls or fences and as close to each other as possible. Such parking configurations make it very difficult to open the doors and steal merchandise.

- If door-to-wall parking is not possible, position the vehicles so that the back end of one truck is flush against the back of another.

- If loaded trailers must be uncoupled from their tractors, especially in freight yards unprotected by fencing, consider the use of kingpin locks. These locks, placed on the kingpin or fifth wheel, prevent thieves from coming in with their own tractor, hooking up the trailer, and making off with the entire load.

- Maintain strict control over the ignition keys to trucks. Do not leave them in parked trucks, even in security-controlled yards. Keys left in vehicles are often taken and copied. Then, when the truck is on the road en route to a delivery and the driver stops to take a break at a truck stop, the entire truck and its contents are stolen. Ignition keys should be controlled by the shipping department supervisor or, at the very least, by the security guard. They should only be released to drivers upon the presentation of valid shipping documents and company identification.

In-Transit Operations

This is the last link in the supply chain: getting the merchandise from the warehouse to the store or, in some cases, from the store to the customer. Unfortunately, it is often the weakest link in the chain. In-transit cargo theft ranges from collusive theft engaged in by dishonest shipping department personnel and drivers to the organized hijacking of the truck and its entire contents. It also includes "grab and run" thefts from unlocked trucks stopped at traffic lights, and unauthorized deliveries and direct thefts caused by dishonest drivers. Such thefts are difficult to control but it can be done.

The biggest percentage of in-transit theft can be stopped before the truck ever hits the road. All truck and trailer cargo doors should be locked and sealed. The locks should be high-security padlocks that are chained to the truck, to prevent lock switching by dishonest drivers. The locking mechanism should be a combination type or a removable core, pin tumbler key type. The driver must not be allowed access to the combination or the key. Predelivery procedures can be established with receiving store managers for the transmission of lock combinations or the delivery of the appropriate keys in sealed envelopes. With effective lock-and-key controls in place, a system can remain in effect for a month or two. The combinations or keys should then be changed, to minimize the threat of their having been compromised.

In addition to locks, high-value cargo should be protected by seals. Cargo seals, commonly referred to as railroad seals (they were first used to protect freight train cargo), are an extremely effective method of detecting unauthorized entry into padlocked areas. They have tremendous deterrent value. When used to secure in-transit cargo, these seals, which are available in a wide variety of metal and plastic configurations, are fastened through the hasp along with the lock. Even if the lock itself is defeated, further entry cannot be made without breaking the seal. They will not stop a nonemployee thief from breaking both the lock and the seal to steal the cargo, but they are very effective in preventing theft by company drivers. To prevent unauthorized access to and switching of seals by dishonest drivers—and, frequently their shipping department cohorts—seals can be numbered and controlled in the same manner as the combinations and key to locks. Examples of some seals used for cargo transport security purposes are shown in Figure 8.1.

FIGURE 8.1　Transportation Seals.

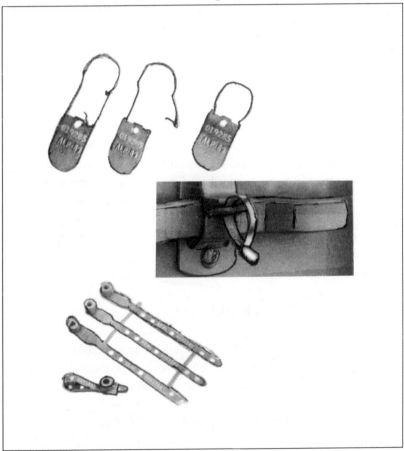

(*Source:* E. J. Brooks Company)

Implementation of the following recommendations should give additional protection:

- Nonstop hauls should be made whenever possible. If drivers must lay over in freight terminals or truck stops, they should be instructed in the security measures necessary to protect their cargo.

- Trucks going to the same destination should travel in convoys. The more people around, the less chance there is for theft to occur.

- When shipments are extremely valuable, consideration should be given to having the truck escorted by a supervisor or security official in a trailing vehicle. The two vehicles should have visual signal systems and CB or other voice communication.

- If movements of very valuable merchandise are frequent, consideration should be given to welding to the bed of one or more delivery trucks special steel boxes that can be locked and alarmed.

- Periodic surveillance of company trucks is strongly recommended. These observations will not only divulge unauthorized stops and activities by drivers, they will also provide an opportunity to examine the driver's adherence to company safe-driving policies. When surveillances are discovered, and they will be, they are of great deterrent value. Once word gets around that trucks are being followed, losses attributable to driver theft are dramatically reduced.

MONETARY CONTROLS

If merchandise is the lifeblood of a retail establishment, money is the only end product that counts. Money represents profit or loss, success or failure. To employees, it is the most tempting of assets to steal, and must therefore be closely monitored and controlled.

Two primary cash-generating and cash-handling operations are highly susceptible to embezzlement by employees: (1) the accounting/bookkeeping function and (2) the cash register or point-of-sale operation. Both must be controlled.

Accounting/Bookkeeping Controls

Separation of Duties

No one person should be in a position or have the authority to make purchases, receive merchandise, *and* pay the bills. Lack of control over all of these critical functions makes embezzlement not only easy, but difficult to detect.

Keep in mind an old security axiom: "The employee you trust the most can steal the most."

Verifications and Approvals

All accounting/bookkeeping work should be reviewed and approved by a supervisor. Invoices, receipts, and other documentation used to support journal entries should also be checked. Periodically, invoices and receipts should be checked with the home offices of vendors, to verify that costs and totals listed have not been "raised" by the delivery person or the bookkeeper.

If you do not make the daily bank deposits yourself, compare the deposits made by employees with the record of cash and checks received. Make sure you get duplicate deposit slip verifications from the bank. Compare them with bookkeeper entries, and personally reconcile all bank statements.

Company Mail

If you regularly receive cash payments, checks, and money orders in the mail, consider having all company mail addressed to a post office box rather than to your store. This system will enable you to better control the receipt, opening, and recording of the contents.

Company Checks

Blank checks and check-writing machines must be safeguarded, and access to them must be closely monitored. Periodically, check the back pages of checkbooks, to ensure that no pages are missing and that the numerical sequence of the checks is intact.

Never sign blank checks. Do not routinely sign checks for merchandise received or repairs ostensibly made, without first examining the invoices and supporting documentation.

188 PREVENTING THEFT BY EMPLOYEES

Audits

A complete financial audit, at periodic intervals, by an outside audit firm is strongly recommended. *Insist that the auditors audit for fraud.* Unfortunately, many auditors only audit for account reconciliation and regulatory compliance. Some of them do not take the extra steps necessary to detect ongoing fraud. One constantly reads newspaper reports of major business embezzlements that have been detected only after they have been going on for long periods of time, in spite of annual audits. These long-term embezzlements were possible because the auditors accepted at face value the documents they were reviewing.

In an audit for fraud, documents must be examined for evidence of alterations and cross-checked with other bookkeeping accounts. Representative samplings and verifications of them must be conducted to ensure their validity. There have been countless cases of embezzlement by innovative company accountants, bookkeepers, and, yes, even managers, who have raised the numbers on invoices or created totally fictitious suppliers and "ghost" employees to cover their depredations. In an audit for fraud, auditors take a number of invoices and verify their validity with the vendors, suppliers, custodial, maintenance, and other firms and individuals named. That is the only sure way that employee embezzlement is likely to be detected. Periodic cross-checks between payroll and personnel records are recommended, to discover any listing of "ghost" employees.

Bonding Firms

If the amount of cash or financial documentation handled by accountants or other key employees is significantly large, you should consider having them bonded. It might also be wise to bond other employees who handle valuable merchandise such as fine jewelry. Bonding, in and of itself, often serves as a deterrent to theft and embezzlement.

Cash Register Controls

Register Readings

Effective register controls begin with daily opening, shift change, and closing register readings. These readings, often referred to as *Z readings,* provide a running total of all transactions that have occurred on a particular cash register or point-of-sale terminal. Separate readings must be taken for each drawer in a multidrawer register.

There should be no gaps in these readings. The closing reading for one day, or shift, should be the opening reading for the next. *These readings should only be taken by store management personnel.* Allowing sales personnel to take readings on their own registers, or to have access to the special register keys necessary to take such readings, makes it infinitely easier for them to embezzle. One of the most common methods for embezzlement occurs when a dishonest employee, who is allowed to take his or her own register reading, closes out the register an hour or so before the actual end of the business day and uses that reading as a "total receipts" figure when turning in the register receipts. The money received from all subsequent sales that may be transacted before the store finally closes is stolen. The register detail tape is temporarily removed, or the second tape used is destroyed.

Accountability

Each employee should operate from and be totally responsible for his or her own register drawer. This will eliminate problems in assessing liability for any shortages, accidental or deliberate, that may arise. Employees who perform rotational duties, such as filling in during lunch breaks, should also be assigned their own separate drawers, with accountable register readings taken as appropriate. Once accountability for a register drawer is delegated to a specific employee, store managers should not open that drawer unless the employee is present. Otherwise, it is impossible to hold that employee responsible for any shortage that may subsequently be discovered. And don't think for a moment that such an operational shortcoming long goes unnoticed by certain opportunistic employees.

Operating Funds

Employees should be provided with a specific amount of cash with which to operate their register drawer. To preclude any future claims of a shortage, they should be instructed to immediately verify the amounts provided.

Managers can utilize this fund to make a simple "honesty" check of an employee by engaging in a practice known as "salting." All you have to do is add a ten-dollar or twenty-dollar bill to the fund and then sit back and wait to see whether the employee reports it.

Checking-In and Checking-Out

To clearly define responsibility, the checking-in and checking-out of a cash register should be a formal, controlled process. This function should be accomplished independently, without the assistance of other employees. Employees should be required to fill out a preprinted form that lists the composition and totals of the day's receipts. The form should have blocks for recording the opening and closing readings, but these figures should not be filled in or available to register operators. An example of a cashier's check-in and check-out form is shown in Figure 8.2.

Managers should bear in mind, when tabulating and checking register receipts received from employees, that not all shortages are the result of theft. Most are purely accidental. And some, humorous only in retrospect, are truly unbelievable. For example, did you hear about the college student who earned most of his tuition by working part-time as a cashier in a sporting goods store? Every evening when checking-out, in order to save time and check his accuracy, he used the cash register as an adding machine. Trying to balance out the register drove the manager absolutely crazy. Or, the part-time check-out clerk in the drug store, who, every time she got a "round" of change, rang it up on the register before she put it in the drawer. Her manager also ended up as a basket case.

Speaking of change, cash register repairs are very costly. Instruct your employees *not* to break open rolls of coins on open register drawers.

Recording Sales

This is where things really get sticky, especially when you are coping with "sticky-fingered" employees. Company policies must clearly state that *all sales are to be rung up immediately and completely and the register drawer is to be closed after every transaction.* Purchases

FIGURE 8.2 Sample Form for Checking Cash Register Receipts.

CASHIER'S CHECK-IN/CHECK-OUT FORM

Date _____

Dept _____

Reg No _____ Drawer _____

Shift _____

Cashier _____

CHECK-IN

Amount of Bank $_____

Pennies	_____
Nickels	_____
Dimes	_____
Quarters	_____
Other Coins	_____
Ones	_____
Fives	_____
Tens	_____
Twenties	_____
Fifties	_____
One Hun'ds	_____
Sub-Total	**$_____**
Over - (Short)	_____

TOTAL CHECK-IN $_____

Signature _____

CHECK-OUT

Pennies	_____
Nickels	_____
Dimes	_____
Quarters	_____
Other Coins	_____
Ones	_____
Fives	_____
Tens	_____
Twenties	_____
Fifties	_____
One Hun'ds	_____
Checks*	_____
Credit Cards*	_____
Chg. Cards*	_____
Other*	_____
Sub-Total	**$_____**

ADJUSTMENTS

Less Overrings*	(_____)
Less Paid-Outs*	(_____)
Other Deducts*	(_____)
Sub-Total	**$_____**
Less Bank	(_____)

TOTAL RECEIPTS $_____

* **Documentary Verification Required**

BOOKKEEPER/MANAGER'S RECONCILIATION

Opening Reading	$_____
Closing Reading	$_____
TOTAL RECORDED	$_____
Total Adjustments	$____(_____)__
AMOUNT TURNED IN	$_____
Amount Over (Short)	$_____

(*Source:* ProTect - Retail Loss Prevention)

should not be combined; each item must be recorded separately. Sales personnel should not be allowed to make any type of adjustment or correct an error by improperly recording the price of the next item. *The customer's receipt must accurately reflect the exact price of each item purchased.* Failure to adhere to these policies allows most register thefts to occur.

Register thefts, often referred to as "knocking-down" and "till-tapping," are accomplished in numerous ways. For example, while operating a busy front check-out register, a cashier leaves her drawer open. As people rush through, she makes change from it, never or only occasionally recording a sale properly. The unregistered money thereby accumulated is later surreptitiously removed. Or, a salesman deliberately underrecords a sale for a customer. After the drawer is opened, he notices the "mistake," recomputes it on a handy scrap of paper, accepts the additional money, and puts it into the register—without recording it. He now has an overage in his register which, of course, he will later take. Or, if he is clever enough and doesn't want to get caught with an overage in his drawer, he passes the overage off as change to an accomplice posing as a customer.

Detecting Register Theft

There are several methods store owners and managers can use to detect and deter thefts from cash registers. Among them are:

- **Alertness.** Managers must look for and be able to recognize indications of possible register manipulation by dishonest employees. Most employees who steal keep a running tally of their "take" so they will know how much to remove when the opportunity presents itself. Look for out-of-place bills or coins in the cash drawer—pennies in the quarters slot, for example, with each penny representing a dollar to be taken. Look around the register for other items that could be used to keep count: a grouping of paper clips, candy, or peanuts, or markings on scraps of paper.

- **Spot checks.** To catch employees who have already pulled money out of a register, which they will subsequently make up for by underringing, or to catch those who have accumulated an overage in the register, which they have not yet removed, nothing can compare with "spot checks." In this procedure, managers take unannounced register readings and count the receipts on hand. Besides being useful for fraud detection, this policy is an extremely effective deterrent.

Use common sense when making spot checks: do not allow a set pattern to develop, such as the practice of making only one each day. Alert and devious employees will soon notice this shortcoming and will wait until after you make your check before they start "knocking down" on their registers. Vary the numbers and the times of your spot checks. Double-back and check the same employee you checked earlier. Put special emphasis on new employees.

- **Over/Short forms.** Another useful procedure that can be a great asset in detecting dishonest cash register operators is the use of an over/short form. This is a simple, calendar-type form on which the performance of all employees over a given period of time, usually a month, is recorded in separate blocks. Overages are recorded in red and shortages in blue, to easily detect patterns and trends. These patterns, especially when erratic, often indicate improper register manipulation. They can also help pinpoint a careless or inept employee who may need additional training or who is so inept that termination is the only solution. An example of an over/short form is shown in Figure 8.3.

Errors and Voids

Register transactions are not always handled perfectly. Employees make mistakes, customers change their minds or, occasionally, discover they do not have enough money to make the intended purchase. The transaction recorded on the register must then be corrected. "Errors," "voids," "overrings," or whatever else you may call them, must be controlled. They are by far the easiest and most common ways for employees to steal from their registers.

The theft is simple. All an employee has to do is pick up a receipt discarded by a customer, mark it "Void," put it in the register drawer

FIGURE 8.3   Sample Form for Recording Cash Register Discrepancies.

CASHIER'S OVER/SHORT FORM
(Blue Ink = Over   Red Ink = Short)

Date: Two-Week Period From _____ to _____

Salesperson														Total Over (Short)

(Source: ProTect - Retail Loss Prevention)

and take out the equivalent amount in cash. Or, if no receipt is available, and depending on store procedures, the employee might complete some unverified form claiming an error was made, note the amount, and put the form in the register. The equivalent amount in cash can then, as in the previous example, be later removed and no one will be the wiser.

Register errors and voids must be verified by store management at the time they occur and while the customer is still present. A formal, two-copy, preprinted form should be utilized. It should indicate the register location or number, the transaction number, and the amount of the error, and it should be signed by both the cashier and the supervisor, with each person who signs retaining a copy. The register detail tape can also be circled and initialed by the supervisor. These forms should not be completed by sales personnel nor should they have access to them. An example of a void/overring form is shown in Figure 8.4.

FIGURE 8.4   Sample Form for Recording Cash Register Voids or Overrings.

VOID/OVERRING FORM

Dept: _____   Date: _____

Register/Drawer No: _____   Transaction No: _____

Salesperson: _____

Amt Mdse Error: _____Tax: ____ Total Error: _____

Reason: _____

Signature Salesperson: _____

Signature Supervisor: _____

**TO BE AUTHORIZED BY SUPERVISOR
WHILE CUSTOMER IS STILL PRESENT**

**Prepare in Duplicate
1 copy to salesperson - 1 copy to supervisor**

(*Source:* ProTect - Retail Loss Prevention)

Because a register receipt must usually be available to engage in cash register embezzlements, additional attention must be focused on controlling their availability. Every effort should be made to ensure that customers receive and leave the store with their receipts. A good practice to institute is to have sales personnel staple the receipt around the carry-area of the bag containing the customer's purchase. Another procedure that will induce customers to take their receipts, and to pay more attention to the manner in which their transactions are recorded, is the use of specially marked register receipt tapes. Tapes are available that are randomly imprinted with company logos or designs such as stars. Signs are posted at cash registers announcing that if a logo or star appears on the customer's receipt, the customer will receive a 10 percent discount. The use of this type of system helps in stemming knocking-down and till-tapping activities as well as preventing fraudulent overrings and voids.

Refund and Exchange Controls

This subject was initially discussed in relation to external loss prevention issues, but it is an equally significant internal control problem and is therefore being mentioned again. Unfortunately, the biggest percentage of all refund fraud is committed by employees. To ensure that this potentially significant drain on your profits is not overlooked in the development of your internal control procedures, you should review, in Chapter 6, the vulnerability concerns and the corrective recommendations regarding refunds. Refer also to the refund/exchange form shown in Figure 6.6.

Sales to Relatives

Employees should be instructed that, in order to keep themselves free from suspicion, they should not handle transactions for members of their immediate family or for relatives.

Professional Shopping Services

Another method of control that can be very effective is to retain the services of a professional shopping firm. Personnel from the firm, posing as regular customers, can evaluate your employees on their courtesy, appearance, job knowledge, and general efficiency. Professional shoppers are usually trained to detect employees engaged in dishonest cash register operations and other improper or illegal activities.

Miscellaneous Operational Controls

Depending on the size and type of your business, the following general controls should be considered for implementation:

- Limit access to the store office and keep it locked when unattended.
- Control the use of store telephones. Allow them to be used for business and personal emergencies only.
- Establish firm policies for the use of company vehicles.
- Do not allow your employees to accept gifts, travel, lodging, or gratuities of any type from any suppliers or vendors from whom they order merchandise or whose shipments or deliveries they are responsible for checking in.

EMPLOYEE TERMINATIONS AND ARRESTS

While admittedly somewhat of a sour note on which to end this chapter, terminations and arrests are, nevertheless, the way some employer–employee relationships are concluded. Which course of action to pursue—termination or arrest—is a judgmental decision that only you can make. The age of the employee involved, the length of employment, and the position held, as well as the amount of money or value of the merchandise stolen, will be mitigating factors. Compassion and "second chances" have their place, but *all significant illegal actions by employees should result in immediate termination and arrest*. This outcome, when shown to be with cause, will have a significant deterrent impact on the rest of your work force.

Terminations and arrests are very complex issues that must be handled with extreme care. The legalistic minefield that must be traversed is very similar to the hazards encountered when dealing with shoplifters. You must be factually sure of what has transpired, you must have the evidence, and you must be certain you are accusing the right employee. Before pursuing any termination or arrest, you would be well advised to reread Chapter 4 on shoplifting and substitute *employee* wherever the word *shoplifter* appears. All of the same caveats apply. Pay particular attention to the discussion of confrontations, detentions, arrests, written statements, the care and control of evidence, and civil releases.

You have some major advantages when dealing with employees rather than shoplifters. You know the identity of your suspect, and you have the luxury of time. In most incidents, particularly those involving embezzlements, you do not have to make an immediate decision. You can get some professional help.

Rarely is employee theft or embezzlement a one-time thing. If it happens once, it is more than likely going to happen again. If your suspicions have been aroused but you are not fully positive about what occurred, you can increase your vigilance so that the next time it happens you will be able to get all of the evidence you need to make an arrest. In fact, in many instances, you will be able to enlist the help of your local police or hire a private investigative firm. Such action is highly recommended.

If you actually catch an employee in the act of stealing your merchandise, your reaction should be swift and sure. Recover the merchandise and decide whether you want to prosecute. If you opt to do so, call the police and let them handle it. *If you decide not to prosecute but to terminate the employee instead, do not do it without first interviewing the employee and getting a written admission of guilt.* You may use the same statement form that was developed for use with shoplifters (see Figure 4.5).

The statement itself need not be lengthy. All you really need is the full identification of the employee, the length of time employed, the position held, and a brief narration of the incident. You also need a listing of the merchandise stolen and the written admission of guilt. The signature of the employee, your signature, and that of a witness complete the document.

If, during the interview, you get an admission that the employee has other stolen company merchandise at another location, have the employee include, in his or her written statement, permission for you to recover it, or have the employee execute a separate Consent to Search (see Figure 4.6). The employee may also admit to the theft of merchandise that is no longer recoverable, such as foodstuffs and other perishables. An itemized listing of this stolen merchandise should be made and its value determined. If, as is usually the case, the employee offers to make full restitution, the list of the merchandise stolen, its value, and the employee's offer of restitution should be included in the written statement. Unless full repayment is made at the time of the interview, the employee should be asked to sign a promissory note to cover the amount of the restitution. An example of a promissory note is shown in Figure 8.5. This form can also be used as a means to recover monetary losses, such as thefts from a cash register, when prosecution is not pursued. After all necessary documents have been signed and witnessed, and before the employee is terminated for a violation of company policy (stealing), have the employee sign a Civil Release (see Figure 4.7) absolving you and the store from any possible civil liability charges if any errors have been made.

In conclusion, I strongly recommend that, before being faced with a termination or arrest, you seek the prior advice of your attorney and ensure that you fully understand your obligations, your rights, and the legal requirements for pursuing such action within your operational jurisdiction. Then, once you understand them, write them down and make them part of your company policy.

FIGURE 8.5   Sample of Promissory Note Form.

PROMISSORY NOTE

Date: _____

County of: _____

State of: _____

On demand, for value received, I, _____,

promise to pay to _____

the sum of _____dollars

in lawful money of the United States, with interest at the rate of _____ percent per annum, interest payable monthly.

In case said interest is not paid when due, it shall be added to the principal and bear a like rate of interest until paid and the whole of said principal and interest shall forthwith become due at the option of the holder hereof without notice.

All sums shall be paid at_____.

The consideration for this note is money owed by me to:

_____

and is not given in exchange for any promise, express or implied, to withhold or stifle criminal prosecution. In case suit is brought to collect this note or any portion thereof, I promise and agree to pay such additional sum as the court may adjudge reasonable for attorney's fees in said action.

_____   _____

Witness   Signature

_____   _____

Address   Address

(*Source:* ProTect - Retail Loss Prevention)

INTERNAL LOSS PREVENTION CHECKLIST

Preventing Employee Theft

- ☐ Train all store managers in the various means used by employees to steal.
- ☐ Develop and implement personnel controls.
- ☐ Develop and implement merchandise controls.
- ☐ Train managers to make a habit of routinely checking trash bins and garbage containers for concealed merchandise.

Warehouse Operations Control

- ☐ Make sure there is sufficient lighting in the warehouse.
- ☐ Make sure lock and alarm systems are adequate.
- ☐ Use convex mirrors and closed-circuit television systems.
- ☐ Control the activities of both employees and nonemployees.

Receiving Department Operations Control

- ☐ Limit the hours of operation.
- ☐ Configure the truck-docking bays so that merchandise cannot be surreptitiously off-loaded and hidden.
- ☐ Accurately count all incoming merchandise.
- ☐ Make sure supervisors spot check incoming merchandise.
- ☐ Instruct receiving clerks to check for inferior product substitutions.
- ☐ Develop procedures for handling of overshipments.
- ☐ Establish a system to properly account for and control returns received from company stores.

(Continued)

(Continued)

Shipping Department Operations Control

- ☐ Make store management aware of the major losses that can occur as a result of uncontrolled shipping department operations.

- ☐ Recognize that not all shipping department losses occur in the shipping department.

- ☐ Make store management aware of the collusive means employees can use—for example, among sales, shipping, warehouse, and delivery personnel—to engage in shipping department theft.

- ☐ Rotate personnel occasionally, to discourage collusion.

- ☐ Make sure every document that is used to authorize, move, or ship merchandise is sequentially numbered and accounted for.

- ☐ Monitor company mailing facilities to avoid misuse.

Transportation Operations Control

- ☐ Make sure the warehouse yard and truck staging area are well lighted and enclosed by secure, alarmed fencing.

- ☐ Use only one gate to the complex.

- ☐ Make sure the gate is controlled by security guards.

- ☐ Once trucks and trailers are loaded, make sure they are locked with high-security padlocks. Give keys only to the shipping department supervisor.

- ☐ Park loaded trucks and trailers so that the doors cannot be easily opened.

- ☐ If trailers must be uncoupled from their tractors in unprotected areas, use kingpin locks to prevent them from being stolen.

(Continued)

☐ Maintain strict control over the ignition keys to the trucks.

In-Transit Operations Control

☐ Lock all truck and trailer cargo doors. In addition, safeguard them by using transportation seals.

☐ Control the keys to truck and trailer cargo doors.

☐ Control the seals.

☐ Require trucks going to the same destination to travel in convoys.

☐ Periodically survey company trucks.

Monetary Controls

☐ Separate the duties of all accounting/bookkeeping functions.

☐ Make sure a supervisor reviews and approves all accounting/bookkeeping work.

☐ Verify bank deposits.

☐ If company mail includes payments in the form of cash, checks, or money orders, have it sent to a postal box rather than to the store's street address.

☐ Safeguard blank checks and check-writing machines and closely monitor access to them.

☐ Make sure complete financial audits are conducted at periodic intervals by an outside audit firm.

☐ Ask the auditors to audit for fraud.

☐ Make sure all accountants, bookkeepers, and other employees who handle valuable merchandise are bonded.

(Continued)

(Continued)

Cash Register Controls

☐ Take daily register readings.

☐ Make sure register readings are taken only by store management personnel.

☐ Assign each employee a specific register drawer.

☐ Verify cash register operating funds when received.

☐ Establish a formal, controlled process for checking-in and checking-out of the registers.

☐ Develop company policies that clearly state that all sales are to be rung up immediately and completely and that the register is to be closed after every transaction.

☐ Make sure store management is alert and able to recognize indications of possible register manipulations by dishonest employees.

☐ Make cash register spot checks of all cashiers.

☐ Use over/short forms to monitor employee register performance.

☐ Develop a formal control procedure for handling voids and overrings.

☐ Make sure errors and voids are verified by store management while the customer is still present.

☐ Develop a formal control procedure for handling returns and exchanges.

Miscellaneous Operational Controls

☐ Control the use of store telephones.

☐ Establish firm policies for the use of company vehicles.

☐ Develop policies prohibiting the acceptance of gifts, travel, lodging, or gratuities from vendors.

(Continued)

Employee Terminations and Arrests

☐ Develop and implement formal policies regarding the termination and arrest of employees who are caught stealing merchandise or embezzling funds.

☐ Have all such policies reviewed by an attorney to ensure legal compliance.

CHAPTER NINE

Conclusion

The implementation of all of the suggestions in this book may at first appear to be a very daunting and time-consuming task; it really isn't. Many of the suggestions can be put into effect by making a simple change in mental attitude and by fostering an increased awareness of loss prevention concerns. Other suggestions will require some careful review, along with changes in procedures, the formulation of policies, and employee training.

Recognize that you have already taken a quantum leap toward the establishment of an effective loss prevention program for your store. The mere fact that you have selected and read this book is indicative of your awareness of the problem and your desire to identify your vulnerabilities. It also reflects your positive attitude regarding the development and implementation of preventive measures. You are well on your way to success. All you have to do now is put all the preventive measures together. Don't try to do it all at once. Take it a step, or a chapter, at a time. Do it logically, in the following order:

- Identify the problems and the vulnerabilities.
- Decide what corrective actions are necessary to rectify each problem.
- Develop the procedures and controls necessary.
- Train and obtain the support of your employees.
- Implement the entire program.

IDENTIFYING PROBLEMS AND VULNERABILITIES

This first, most critical step will serve as your "road map." Remember, unless you know where a leak in your system is coming from, you're not going to be able to stop it. Helping you with the task of identifying your vulnerabilities has been the purpose of this entire book. Each chapter has concluded with a checklist designed to assist you in developing a particular phase of your loss prevention program. Make copies of these checklists, and take them on a walk around your store. Use the checklists as handy references to identify all of the vulnerabilities and issues you want to address. Don't get discouraged if your "to do" list gets a little long. Recognize it as evidence that you are doing a thorough, honest job of analysis. Besides, think how good you'll feel when you correct each problem you have identified.

PLANNING AND DECISION MAKING

After you have completed your assessment of what needs to be done, your next course of action is: "How should I do it?" The answer depends on the problem. Most problems, fortunately, are going to be self-evident. If you have a physical security problem, you may need to upgrade your locks and alarm systems. If your problem is an internal one, such as a lack of adequate procedural controls, new policies will have to be written and, in many cases, forms developed. This time-consuming but rewarding exercise will have to be factored into your decision-making process.

DEVELOPING PROCEDURES
AND CONTROLS

The development of procedures and controls is, by its very nature, a thought-provoking and time-consuming task. It will force you to take a very close look at the way you conduct your business and to see things in a way that you haven't seen them before. For example, in developing a loss prevention control policy, you will be required to put yourself in the position of a potential thief and ask yourself, "How can I beat this system?" Every time you come up with a way to beat your own system, you will be challenged to develop a control procedure to prevent it. This will be particularly true in the development of your internal control policies. Start with the development of your general company rules and regulations, and then work your way through every operational facet of your business.

TRAINING AND MOTIVATING EMPLOYEES

Unless you have a well-trained and motivated work force, your business will flounder; in fact, it could very well sink. Hundreds of books have been written on training employees. Get and review some of them. The time spent will be well worth the investment.

As an alternative to obtaining the relevant knowledge and training your employees yourself, you can retain the services of a professional retail loss prevention consultant. These outside specialists generally make a very favorable impression on employees, for two very good reasons: (1) they provide graphic evidence that the store owner is serious about loss prevention, and (2) they can field a wide variety of questions and provide guidance concerning issues that are usually beyond the experience of most store managers. The consultants are also exceptionally valuable for conducting overall security and loss prevention evaluations of individual stores and for providing in-depth loss prevention training for supervisory personnel.

Regardless of how you conduct the actual training, as you initiate the planning and development of your loss prevention program, let your employees know what is going on. Bring them into the process at an early stage. If you feel that significant changes will be required, or even if you just want to put increased emphasis on security and loss prevention issues, a meeting with your entire work force is strongly recommended. You must get them to understand your motivation and enlist their cooperation. This is especially important when the subject of internal controls is addressed. Let them take part in and contribute to the process.

Fortunately, most employees are honest, law-abiding citizens who are sincerely interested in doing a good job. Along with their concern about their job security, they also have a realistic understanding of the many difficulties and problems inherent in the successful and continued operation of a retail establishment. Most of them, in fact, view their situation quite simply:

No profit, no store!

No store, no job!

IMPLEMENTING THE ENTIRE PROGRAM

This is it. You have worked very hard. You now have everything you need to institute your own loss prevention program. You have the desire, the knowledge, the plans, policies and procedures, and a well-trained and motivated staff. You have it all together. Your task now is to implement the entire program to ensure that it has all been worthwhile, that all of your work has not been in vain. Don't forget that a lot of people are depending on you—your family and your employees. They are relying on you for their personal safety and their financial well-being. Don't let them down.

You can do it. Look how far you have already come. The implementation of a strong and formal loss prevention program in your store is important, necessary, and can be accomplished. Go for it!

Good luck. May you and your business prosper!

APPENDIX

Sources for Locks, Alarms, and Security Devices

The following listing of lock, alarm, and security device manufacturers, distributors, and systems providers is furnished for reference purposes only. It is, by no means, all-inclusive. Additional product information can be obtained by reviewing the *Thomas Register,* in the reference section of your local library; by examining your local telephone directories; and by consulting with the professional, licensed locksmiths and security device installation firms servicing your local area.

ACCESS SYSTEMS

Locks

American Lock Co.
2400 W. Exchange Road
Crete, IL 60417
Tel: 708-534-2000

Arrow Lock Mfg. Co.
103-00 Foster Avenue
Brooklyn, NY 11236
Tel: 718-257-4700

Kenstan Lock Co.
166 West Hills Road
Huntington Station, NY 11746
Tel: 516-271-2700

Kwikset Corp.
516 E. Santa Ana Street
Anaheim, CA 92803
Tel: 714-535-8111

LOCKNETICS Security Eng.
575 Birch Street
Forestville, CT 06010
Tel: 203-584-9158

Master Lock Co.
2600 N. 32nd Street
Milwaukee, WI 53210
Tel: 414-444-2800

Medeco High Security Locks
P.O. Box 3075
Salem, VA 24153
Tel: 703-380-5000

Sargent & Greenleaf, Inc.
1 Security Drive
Nicholasville, KY 40356
Tel: 606-885-9411

Sargent Manufacturing Co.
100 Sargent Drive
New Haven, CT 06511
Tel: 202-562-2151

Schlage Lock Co.
2401 Bayshore Blvd.
San Francisco, CA 94134
Tel: 415-467-1100

SECURITECH Group Inc.
54-45 44th Street
Maspeth, NY 11378
Tel: 1-800-622-5625

Simplex Access Controls
2941 Indiana Avenue
Winston-Salem, NC 27115
Tel: 910-725-1331

Yale Security Inc.
P.O. Box 25288
Charlotte, NC 28212
Tel: 704-283-2101

Time Locks

Silent Watchman
2461 McGaw Road
Columbus, OH 43207
Tel: 614-491-5200

Simplex Time Recorder Co.
Simplex Plaza
Gardner, MA 01441
Tel: 1-800-221-7336

Key Controls

Key Systems Inc.
948 Culver Road
Rochester, NY 14609
Tel: 716-654-9388

Secura Key
20447 Nordhoff Street
Chatsworth, CA 91311
Tel: 1-800-891-0020

Transportation Seals

E. J. Brooks Co.
164 N. 13th Street
Newark, NJ 07107
Tel: 1-800-458-7325

Sales—Distributors

Safemasters
National Industrial Sales
5655 General Washington Drive
Alexandria, VA 22312
Tel: 1-800-633-9977

ALARMS

Equipment

ADEMCO
165 Eileen Way
Syosset, NY 11791
Tel: 1-800-645-7492

Alarm Lock Systems, Inc.
345 Bayview Avenue
Amityville, NY 11701
Tel: 1-800-252-5625

System Providers

ADT Security Systems, Inc.
1 Boca Place—2255 Glades Rd.
Boca Raton, FL 33431
Tel: 407-997-8406

Honeywell Protection Services
37-08 Greenpoint Avenue
Long Island City, NY 11101
Tel: 718-361-2828

Wells Fargo Alarm Services
780 Fifth Avenue
King of Prussia, PA 19406
Tel: 215-337-3855

SURVEILLANCE EQUIPMENT

Closed-Circuit Television

VICON Industries, Inc.
525 Broad Hollow Road
Melville, NY 11747
Tel: 1-800-229-1996

Lester L. Brossard Co.
P.O. Box 708
Woodstock, IL 60098
Tel: 815-338-7825

Mirrors

Bell Glass & Mirror Co.
896 Coney Island Avenue
Brooklyn, NY 11218
Tel: 718-633-4000

SECURITY DEVICES

Cash Protection (Vaults)

Perma-Vault Safe Corp.
P.O. Box 473
Huntington Valley, PA 19006
Tel: 215-364-0330

Theft Deterrent (Shoplifting)

Sensormatic Electronic Corp.
500 Northwest 12th Avenue
Deerfield Beach, FL 33442
Tel: 305-427-9700

Cash Protection (Money Trap)

Linear
2055 Corte Del Nogal
Carlsbad, CA 92009
Tel: 1-800-421-1587

Index